How to
Listen to Your Dog

The Complete Guide to Communicating
with Man's Best Friend

CARLOTTA COOPER

How to Listen to Your Dog: The Complete Guide to Communicating with Man's Best Friend

Copyright © 2015 by Atlantic Publishing Group, Inc.
1405 SW 6th Ave. • Ocala, Florida 34471 • 800-814-1132 • 352-622-1875–Fax
Website: www.atlantic-pub.com • E-mail: sales@atlantic-pub.com
SAN Number: 268-1250

Library of Congress Cataloging-in-Publication Data

Cooper, Carlotta, 1962-
How to listen to your dog : the complete guide to communicating with man's best friend / by Carlotta Cooper.
pages cm
Includes bibliographical references and index.
ISBN 978-1-60138-596-3 (alk. paper) -- ISBN 1-60138-596-X (alk. paper)
1. Dogs--Psychology. 2. Dogs--Behavior. 3. Human-animal communication. I. Title.
SF427.C825 2012
636.7'0835--dc23
2012025440

A few years back we lost our beloved pet dog Bear, who was not only our best and dearest friend but also the "Vice President of Sunshine" here at Atlantic Publishing. He did not receive a salary but worked tirelessly 24 hours a day to please his parents.

Bear was a rescue dog who turned around and showered myself, my wife, Sherri, his grandparents Jean, Bob, and Nancy, and every person and animal he met (well, maybe not rabbits) with friendship and love. He made a lot of people smile every day.

We wanted you to know a portion of the profits of this book will be donated in Bear's memory to local animal shelters, parks, conservation organizations, and other individuals and nonprofit organizations in need of assistance.

– Douglas & Sherri Brown

PS: We have since adopted two more rescue dogs: first Scout, and the following year, Ginger. They were both mixed golden retrievers who needed a home.

Want to help animals and the world? Here are a dozen easy suggestions you and your family can implement today:

- *Adopt and rescue a pet from a local shelter.*
- *Support local and no-kill animal shelters.*
- *Plant a tree to honor someone you love.*
- *Be a developer — put up some birdhouses.*
- *Buy live, potted Christmas trees and replant them.*
- *Make sure you spend time with your animals each day.*
- *Save natural resources by recycling and buying recycled products.*
- *Drink tap water, or filter your own water at home.*
- *Whenever possible, limit your use of or do not use pesticides.*
- *If you eat seafood, make sustainable choices.*
- *Support your local farmers market.*
- *Get outside. Visit a park, volunteer, walk your dog, or ride your bike.*

Five years ago, Atlantic Publishing signed the Green Press Initiative. These guidelines promote environmentally friendly practices, such as using recycled stock and vegetable-based inks, avoiding waste, choosing energy-efficient resources, and promoting a no-pulping policy. We now use 100-percent recycled stock on all our books. The results: in one year, switching to post-consumer recycled stock saved 24 mature trees, 5,000 gallons of water, the equivalent of the total energy used for one home in a year, and the equivalent of the greenhouse gases from one car driven for a year.

Dedication

This book is lovingly dedicated to all the dogs
who have taught me so much in my life.

Acknowledgments

I would like to thank all of the wonderful dog owners, breeders, and trainers who responded to my request and completed case studies for this book. There was an enormous response, and it was impossible to use every reply, but I sincerely appreciate everyone who took the time to fill out the questionnaires.

Thanks to Gretchen Pressley for all her work with this book and the others we have worked on together. She has been a terrific editor and a pleasure to work with over the last couple of years.

Finally, thanks to my good friend Donna. When my computer died halfway through writing this book, she generously loaned me a computer so I could complete my work. Not only that, but she is just an all-around great friend. Thanks, Donna.

Table of Contents

Chapter 2: Ways We Communicate with Our Dogs

Chapter 6: Behavior Problems of Puppies 181

Chapter 7: Behavior Problems of Adult Dogs 201

Chapter 8: Advanced Communication 229

Chapter 9: Communicating with Senior Dogs 259

Introduction

Americans genuinely love dogs. There are an estimated 78 million pet dogs in the U.S. today.

Being able to communicate with your dog greatly improves the quality of life you share together. When you can communicate with your dog and understand what he is trying to tell you, you can avoid behavior problems, which are one of the main reasons so many dogs end up in shelters. Being able to communicate with your dog can save his life.

Training is one of the best ways to improve your communication with your dog. Training provides a way for you and your dog to develop a shared language of obedience commands so you and your dog have the same expectations. Your dog learns ways to please you, which makes him happy. Training allows you and your dog to develop a closer commitment and bond with each other.

Besides obedience training, dogs can excel in many other fields with their human partner: agility, rally, canine freestyle (dog dancing), flyball, Frisbee®, dock diving (water sports), earthdog, hunting, weight pulling, and many other dog sports and activities give people and their dogs a chance to have fun together and do things that they both love to do. In addition, dogs and their human partners can dedicate themselves to important work such as search and rescue, arson detection, and becoming therapy dog teams. None of these things would be possible without good communication between dogs and their people.

Ultimately, communication improves the human-dog bond. When you can look at your dog and know what he is thinking by reading his body language or looking at the way he moves his eyes, then you and your dog are communicating better. It deepens the bond between you and your dog. It gives you insights into how your dog feels and thinks. You can even learn to give your dog signals so he can understand you better. That kind of communication is good for all dogs and their people.

How will you know when you and your dog are achieving good communication? One way is if your dog looks at you and you know what he wants just by the tilt of his head or the way he moves his body. Good communication means you understand what your dog's body language is telling you. You can watch your dog playing with another dog and suddenly see things happening between them that you never noticed before. You start to understand why dogs do some of the things they do. And, of course, you and your dog should be getting along better, too, because you will understand things from your dog's perspective. You should be able to adjust your own signals so your dog can understand you more easily, too.

Author's Story

I got my first Irish setter when I was 12 in 1974. He was a complete heathen of a dog, and I do not think anyone ever tried to train him. It was not until the 1980s that I became seriously interested in dogs. In 1987, I got an English setter puppy as a pet, and I was smitten. I have had English setters since that time, breeding them, showing them, doing some training at home and taking a few classes, sending dogs out to get hunting, obedience, rally, and agility titles for others. I do not breed often, but I have had nice dogs. I currently have five English setters who give me a reason for getting up every morning.

Over the last 25 years, I have learned a lot about communicating with dogs, from naughty puppies to rescue dogs with separation anxiety — from obnoxious stud dogs to elderly dogs trying to hide their ailments. I have been fortunate to share my life with some wonderful dogs that were good at communication.

For a long time in the 1990s, most of my dogs were dogs that I bred myself. I was with them from the time they were born, so it seemed to me that communication with them was easy. They learned everything from me from the time they first opened their eyes. Even their mothers were attuned to me, so we were all speaking the same "language," so to speak. The dogs, of all ages, and I used the same words for everything. We all knew the same body language. I knew their body language, and they knew mine. So, for a couple of generations of dogs I never thought much about communication because it almost seemed intuitive with us. I also felt like I was preparing my puppies for what they needed to know before they went to live with their new families.

Then I took a break from showing and breeding for about five years, and I did not have any puppies during this time. And when I wanted to have a puppy again, I had to go to another breeder to get one instead of breeding my own. That puppy was Billie. I did not think too much about communication with Billie, but I wonder now if maybe I did not teach Billie all the communication skills she needed to learn. I think she does have some communication problems now. She is sociable but not as "communicative" as my other dogs.

Then, a couple years later, I wanted to get another puppy, Pearl. With Pearl, I was aware from the start that we needed to develop a common language. I tried to communicate with her the same way I communicated with my adult dogs — the dogs that I had bred myself and which I could communicate with so easily — and I realized that if I wanted to communicate that way with Pearl, we were going to have to work at it. Luckily, Pearl is a smart dog and she started learning fast. Somehow, we became close, and she can almost read my mind now. But it did not start out that way. At first, it was like trying to communicate with someone from a foreign land. I realized that we did not share the same words or language. We did not know each other's body language. I think part of it was just spending time together and learning about each other.

I think people can develop this kind of understanding and communication in different ways. You can learn with your dog, step by step. You can raise a puppy from birth. And sometimes you can miss an opportunity to develop good communication skills with your dog if you do not work at it.

I do talk things over with Pearl and my other dogs. I learn from her all the time. Sometimes I almost forget she is a dog, and I expect her to answer me when I am talking to her or thinking about her. Dogs can have a large vocabulary, and they seem to understand a great deal of what we say to them, both key words and the overall meaning. It is not just the tone of your voice your dog can understand. They understand certain words you use in your sentences, especially if you use particular phrases every day.

My dogs seem to be good at language, perhaps because I talk to them so much. They know all kinds of words and phrases for things. They also know words for certain activities. If I say, "Let's go watch TV," they all head off to the room where we watch TV before I take a step, so they can curl up next to me while I watch TV. They know what it means when I say, "I'm going to get the mail." Or at least they know that I am going to go out the front door. But that statement does not get the same kind of excited reaction that I get when I pick up my keys and purse and head to the door. They know those actions mean I am leaving the house for a longer time. They know "food," "breakfast," and "hungry" for getting fed in the morning. They have learned "fish oil" now because I have started giving them fish oil gel tabs as treats and using the words. I think they have a pretty big vocabulary. That does not include the words they know for commands such as "sit" and "come."

You would probably be surprised by how many words most pet dogs know. *In Chapter 2, we will look at a dog named Rico who knows more than 200 words for objects.* Some dogs that have been tested know more than 1,000 words.

That is the subject matter of this book: how our dogs communicate with us and how we communicate with them. Sometimes we have miscommunication with our dogs, and this book will help you discover what we can do to improve these misunderstandings. I hope *How To Listen To Your Dog: The Complete Guide To Communicating With Man's Best Friend* will answer your questions and help you develop better communication with your dog.

The Evolution of the Dog and the Dog-Human Relationship

Dogs have been sharing their lives with us since they were first domesticated some 15,000 years ago. According to the archaeological record, dogs probably began to diverge from

wolves about 100,000 years ago, though it is not known if this was due to human influence. The earliest dog-like skull found in a human cave settlement dates to about 32,000 years ago in Belgium, though the skull seems to be somewhere between a dog and wolf in structure. Another dog-like skull was recently discovered in Siberia dating to 33,000 years ago. Humans probably began domesticating these early wolf-dogs about 30,000 years ago, and it was likely a long process that happened in different places at different times. By 16,000 years ago, however, remains that are recognizably like those of modern dogs start to appear in hunter-gatherer settlements, making dogs the earliest of all domesticated animals. Most researchers agree that the dog was probably first permanently domesticated in Southeast Asia, according to DNA evidence.

There are two theories as to how and why these prehistoric dogs that were descended from wolves decided to live with humans. One theory suggests that early humans observed how effective prehistoric dogs were as hunters and took the opportunity to bring home puppies to gentle them so they could teach the dogs to work for them as hunters. Or, perhaps they found puppies and thought they were cute, the way children sometimes bring home a young wild animal and ask their mother if they can keep it. These puppies might have grown up to be socialized and comparatively gentle while working for the hunters. Another theory suggests that prehistoric dogs became interested in humans because of their trash. Wherever there are humans, there is garbage. Hunter-gatherer societies would discard bones, perhaps with meat on them, and sometimes other food. They offered the warmth of fire on cold nights. Early dogs might have followed these humans around to go through the trash looking for food. They might have learned to take handouts of food, and dogs that had a steady supply of food reproduced better, perhaps leading to puppies more willing to socialize with humans. The dogs that had less fear could approach the humans for more food, becoming more socialized. With either scenario, humans would be selecting dogs that were easier to handle, less fearful of them, and more willing to work for them. True domestication would take generations, but these are ways the process could have started.

The Development of Communication with Dogs

So, how did these early humans learn to communicate with these dogs, which were genuinely wild animals? Although we cannot go back in time and observe their interaction or ask our ancient ancestors how they communicated with these wolf-dogs, there have been some recent studies comparing how wolves and dogs learn and communicate that provide some insight into this area.

A recent study led by researcher Monique Udell seems to confirm that dogs are good at reading human expressions and body language, some dogs more than others. The study, published in *Learning & Behavior*, suggests that the more time dogs and other canines spend with people, the better these skills become. The study suggests that this canine understanding might stem from a hyperawareness of the senses.

Udell and a team from the University of Florida wanted to find out how dogs were so good at reading people and their mental and emotional states. They wanted to know if they were born with these abilities or learned them from experience. Udell and her team conducted two different experiments involving begging for food. In both experiments, the animals could either beg from an attentive person or from a person unable to see the begging animal.

The study involved three separate groups of animals: pet dogs, strays from a shelter, and hand-raised wolves that were comfortable with people. Two people stood about 20 feet apart. One person looked directly and continually at the dog or wolf. The other person in the experiment had his vision blocked, either by reading a book or having a bucket over his head, or he turned his back on the dog. But both people had a piece of food.

According to Udell, both the dogs and the wolves were much more likely to beg for food from the person looking at them and making eye contact than from the person turned away. However, there was a difference between the groups of animals and how domesticated their actions seemed. The domesticated dogs were more likely to seek food from someone looking at them. The dogs from shelters and the wolves that did not see someone reading a book often did not pick up on that cue. This suggests that the life experiences of the dog or wolf make a difference in what they understand about communication.

According to the researchers, these findings are important because earlier research had suggested that something happened to dogs when they became domesticated that made them think more like humans. But this study shows that wolves are able to pick up on human cues if they are raised with humans.

This study led its researchers to believe canines are born with the ability to distinguish a human's attentional state and to behave in accordance with it; they can read our cues. Both dogs and wolves have natural people-reading skills, though spending time with humans gives them practice at reading the cues and helps them become better at it.

This kind of study helps us understand how early humans developed communication with early dogs. The key element is that dogs and humans are social animals. Communication is important to both species. From the start of the relationship between early dogs and early humans, dogs must have been willing to accept humans as social companions and learn their body language. They had to be able and willing to learn attentional cues, the contexts for commands, and to consider previous experiences in order for communication to develop. These early wolf-dogs had to be quite remarkable as a species from the start to make this kind of leap and share their lives with humans. Humans, too, had to learn the body language, expressions, and actions of the wolf-dogs to communicate with them — no small accomplishment for early humans who are not usually credited with being the most sensitive of people.

Overview of the Book

Good communication with your dog can improve your relationship and strengthen the bond between you. Being able to understand and communicate with your dog can help you avoid or solve many common behavior problems.

How to Listen to Your Dog: The Complete Guide to Communicating with Man's Best Friend will help you achieve better communication with your dog.

Chapters 1 and 2 will examine ways our dogs communicate with us and ways we communicate with our dogs. These chapters will cover body language, eyes, facial expressions, vocalization, as well as the tools we use such as collars and leashes, training devices, and treats and rewards.

Chapter 3 covers socialization for your puppy or adult dog. The importance of socialization cannot be overemphasized. For puppies, this is the first "training" they receive away from their mothers. Socialization helps to form a dog's personality and can determine how they interact with humans. This chapter also will look at the developmental stages in a puppy's life so you know what to expect at each step along the way.

Chapter 4 will look at how you can learn to communicate effectively with your dog through training. It will examine the different training methods used today, including their pros and cons, and help you choose a method that will work for you and your dog.

Chapter 5 covers basic obedience training and how training can improve your communication with your dog. Teaching your dog basic obedience commands is a good way to build a shared vocabulary.

Chapter 6 will go over some of the behavior problems that are common to puppies. Many owners complain about puppies that chew on inappropriate items (think shoes, remotes, eyeglasses, and purses); puppies jump on people; and they have housetraining issues. Most of the time, these problems occur because the puppy does not know better and has not been trained properly. With a little patience and better communication, these problems are easily fixed.

Chapter 7 will cover some of the behavior problems found in adult dogs such as barking, digging, separation anxiety, and aggression. These problems can be hard to stop in some cases, but improved understanding and communication will help solve them.

Chapter 8 will examine some of the things you can do with your dog when you achieve more advanced levels of communication. Dog organizations offer thousands of events each year for people who enjoy obedience, rally, Frisbee, flyball, musical freestyle (dancing dogs), dock dogs (water sports), herding, hunting, earthdog activities, weight pulling, tracking, and many other sports and activities. There are also jobs for dogs and their owners as therapy dog teams and search and rescue teams, among other things. There is literally almost no limit to the things you and your dog can do if you have good communication.

Chapter 9 will consider some of the ways that aging can affect your dog and alter your ways of communicating with each other. The chapter also will offer some solutions for these issues so you can continue to enjoy and improve your communication with your senior dog.

Finally, the book has an Appendix of resources so you can learn more about dog training and some of the other ideas mentioned in these pages. In addition, I have included sidebars throughout the book called  Author Experiences to share with you some of my dogs that have exemplified certain behaviors or relate stories of my dogs that help illustrate the behavior or training I am describing in that chapter. There are also some interesting case studies from dog owners and trainers who have experiences that shed light on the topics discussed in the book.

For many people, dogs are like beloved family members, yet you might not always know what your dog is trying to tell you. I hope by reading *How to Listen to Your Dog: The Complete Guide to Communicating with Man's Best Friend,* you will learn to communicate better with your dog. You can start improving your communication with your dog by learning the ways dogs communicate with humans in the next chapter.

CHAPTER ONE

Ways Our Dogs Communicate with Us

Wolves and dogs evolved to live in complex social groups known as packs. Packs are organized according to status, familial relationship, usefulness to the group, and other factors. As carnivores, dogs are equipped with teeth that can rip flesh and claws that can injure. Inside the pack, it is important for them to be able to notice and identify subtle changes in body language, eye glances, and facial expressions so they can avoid miscommunications that could lead to fights. Pack members that are always fighting with each other will not survive long in the wild. A certain degree of peace and harmony is necessary for pack survival, and this can only be accomplished with good communication.

A mother canine has to be able to communicate with her pups. She raises them for weeks and teaches them what they need to learn. In the wild, the entire pack will help rear the young and teach them. Young wolves and dogs commonly stay with the pack for months or years in the wild and develop a family structure; they communicate with other members of the pack and understand social roles.

Over the course of thousands of years, dogs have come to look upon humans as their surrogate pack members. They come into our homes and seem to accept us almost immediately in place of their mother and littermates. No other animal accepts us so thoroughly or bonds with us so completely.

When a puppy comes to live with you, he does not know much. What he does know, he has learned from his mother and littermates in a few short weeks. Most puppies go to their new homes between 8 and 12 weeks of age. He has only learned the basics of being a dog at this time, including dog communication skills. He does have canine instincts, however, and by following these instincts, he will display most of the kinds of behaviors, postures, and expressions you will see in adult dogs.

Body Language

Whether you have a new puppy or you have adopted an adult dog from a shelter, you will see similar body language in your dog because canine body language is based on your dog's instincts. In the same way, humans display similar body language around the world. A dog will show happiness, fear, and alertness in similar ways no matter where he is from, what his age is, or other differences.

Most of us with dogs are reasonably good at reading a dog's body language. Humans might be hardwired to understand animals and to recognize when they are dangerous as a preservation skill. In one study, babies just 6 months old were able to tell the difference between snarling dogs and friendly dog sounds when they were played sounds and shown pictures of the dogs using the corresponding body language. The study was conducted by researchers at Brigham Young University and published in the journal, *Developmental Psychology*. Dogs were chosen for the study because the researchers considered them highly communicative in their posture and in their barking.

In the experiment, the babies were first shown two different pictures of the same dog. In one picture, the dog was posing in an aggressive posture, and in the other, the dog was in a friendly pose. Then the researchers played, in random order, sound clips of an aggressive bark and a friendly bark. The babies were only given one trial so they would not learn and figure out what was happening. While the recordings were played, the babies spent most of their time staring at the correct pictures. Older babies typically made an immediate connection between the sound and the image with their first glance.

Most of us probably can tell the difference between a friendly dog and a threatening dog in a split second if the dog approaches us, but we would have a hard time explaining our thought process or describing how we knew the dog was dangerous. Sometimes human instinct takes over, and we recognize canine body language without thinking it through.

Dogs have a multitude of postures and can convey countless messages with their body language. However, every dog owner should learn to recognize some basic signals. There would probably be fewer dog bites and other problems in communities if everyone could recognize these basic postures.

Author Experiences: Julie

If ever a dog had body language that was easy to read, it was Julie. Julie was born being the top dog. Even as a puppy, she dominated her siblings, though she did so without ever doing anything mean. She was exceptionally smart, and she learned everything I taught her fast. Her entire litter was smart, which can probably be credited to their parents. They also had sunny, outgoing dispositions. Julie was outgoing and seemed to naturally expect people to pet her and make a fuss over her. She learned the things a show dog should learn by the time she was only two or three months old. By the time she was 5 ½ months old, she won Best Puppy in Match over 98 other puppies. She had that indefinable quality people talk about when they say someone has "star quality." She was easy and fun to show, and she finished her championship before she was 2 years old in limited showing.

As far as her body language went, she would walk with her head up and her tail out. I never heard her growl or get into a fight, but she did not have to. She could walk into a room, and the other dogs would get down off the furniture so she could have the best spot. There was no question that she was a natural leader. She was just born that way. She is the kind of dog that dog breeders dream about: strong, confident, and happy.

Posture

A wagging tail usually means a dog is happy, but not always. People can recognize puppies at play. If you see a dog snarling and baring his teeth, you know that is a warning and you should back off. But dogs also can show more complex body language. Here are some things you can watch for in your dog:

Happy: If your dog is feeling happy and friendly, he will have his head held high with his mouth relaxed. His ears will be up and interested. His tail will be down and might be wagging.

Alert: If your dog is alert and interested in what is happening, it means he has not yet decided how he should behave. He could act this way when he is meeting a new dog, for example. His ears will be up and his mouth closed. He will be standing up on his toes. His tail will be straight out. He is ready for whatever might happen.

Fearful: A fearful dog might lower his front end. His ears will be back. His nose may wrinkle, and the corner of his mouth might be drawn back. The pupils of his eyes might be dilated. His hackles will be raised. His tail might be tucked in. You should be careful of a fearful dog because frightened dogs can feel threatened, and they might become aggressive. Fearful dogs can bite.

Aggressive: An aggressive dog shows a confident posture. He stands tall and forward on his toes. His ears are forward. His nose is wrinkled and the corner of his mouth is forward.

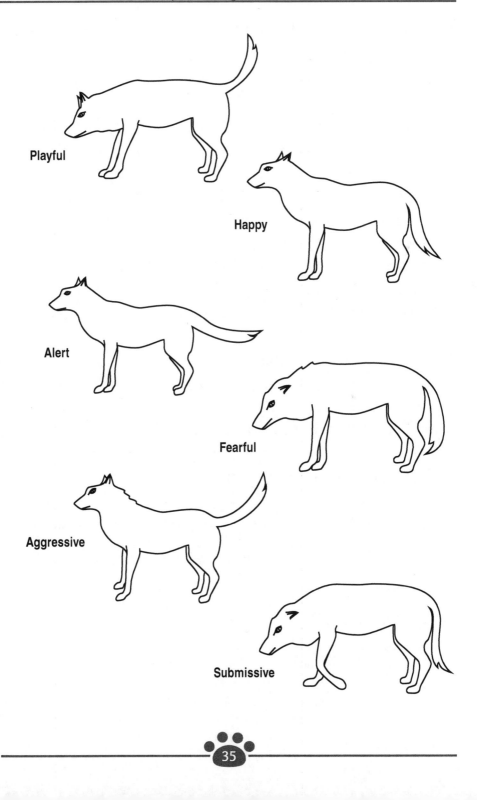

Playful

Happy

Alert

Fearful

Aggressive

Submissive

His hackles are up. His tail is up and stiff. This kind of dog is dangerous, and he can attack. He might growl or bark. He might wag his tail slowly, but this is not a friendly dog.

Submission: A dog might show submission in two ways. He might show active submission by crouching or groveling. His ears are back and his forehead is smooth. He licks at the mouth of another dog. The corners of his mouth are back. Dogs like this might urinate or whine when another dog confronts them. His tail is down and his body is low to the ground. A dog might show passive submission by lying down on his back. He does not make eye contact with the other dog. His tail is tucked to him. This is the most submissive posture for a dog.

Playful: Your dog can show that he wants to play by being excited and happy. He might make a play bow. This is an invitation to another dog to play with him. He will lower his front end and bow with his tail up in the air and wagging. He might run in circles and bark. His ears will be up or slightly back. His hackles are smooth and down.

If your dog is feeling stressed, he might show signs such as:

- Avoiding eye contact or freezing in place
- Diarrhea
- Dilated pupils
- Excessive blinking

- 🐾 Excessive shedding

- 🐾 Hiding behind you

- 🐾 Lack of appetite

- 🐾 Licking his lips

- 🐾 Pacing, restlessness, or becoming agitated or distracted

- 🐾 Panting and salivating

- 🐾 Requiring lots of commands when he usually responds to the first command

- 🐾 Scratching

- 🐾 Shaking

- 🐾 Sniffing

- 🐾 Whining or lots of vocalizing

These are the basic forms of body language that you might see in a dog and what they usually indicate, but there are many variations on these postures, and it is always important to consider context when you are interacting with a dog. You might expect a dog to be happy and friendly when he is playing. Remember that a wagging tail does not always indicate a friendly dog, especially in a tense situation. Fortunately, most people have good instincts when it comes to interacting with dogs. If you are ever in doubt about whether you should go near a dog, it is usually best to be cautious.

Eye contact

You can tell a great deal about a dog's intentions by looking at his eyes. Do not stare into the eyes of a dog you do not know. In fact, you should probably not stare into most dogs' eyes. Dogs interpret a stare as a challenge. If you have a dog that wants to prove he is in charge, you will end up in a staring match. If you have a more submissive  dog, you will make him unhappy and more submissive. Dogs that stare back at your eyes are being bold, though they are not necessarily being aggressive. You could have a good relationship with your dog, and your dog is simply confident. However, staring into the eyes of an unfamiliar dog is the same as issuing a challenge to the dog.

Here are some of the things you can learn to recognize by looking at a dog's eyes:

Happy: A playful, happy dog will have eyes that are wide open and sparkling. His entire face will seem to be more relaxed than usual.

Alert: An alert dog will have eyes that are open to their normal position or a little wider. He looks watchful.

Fearful: A fearful dog has narrow eyes averted away from you. His eyes might be rolled back slightly with the whites showing. His entire posture will give an impression of being tense.

Aggressive: An aggressive dog will have eyes that are narrowed or staring at you in a challenging manner.

Submission: A dog that is feeling submissive can have his eyes either narrowed or wide open, depending on the dog. He probably will be on the ground with his tail tucked. This dog is clearly expressing the idea, "Don't hurt me."

Play: A playful dog will have eyes wide open, and his face will seem relaxed. He might be panting.

Stressed: A dog that is stressed will have his eyes slightly narrowed. He might be in a tense posture that is somewhat submissive.

Dogs are also experts at reading human eye movements and glances. *More on this in Chapter 2.*

Author Experiences: Molly

Molly was another Irish setter. I bought Molly at a pet store because she was outgrowing her cage, and I felt sorry for her. I know I am not the only person who has bought a dog at a pet store out of pity, but Molly seemed to be proof that a good dog could come from anywhere. She lived a long life, and she was never sick. She was possibly the smartest dog I have ever had. When it came to behavior, her only problem was that she enjoyed showing off how smart she was. On one occasion, for instance, I was sound asleep on a Saturday morning when Molly started barking at the front door. Of course, I got up to see if someone was at the door. There was no one there. But, when I returned to the bedroom, there was Molly stretched out in my bed, with her head on my pillow, smirking at me with a twinkle in her eye. I was convinced that she planned the whole episode just to trick me out of bed. And she did not mind gloating about it. I think she was clearly communicating with me at that moment, sharing her little joke with me. I had to laugh at her and myself.

Facial expressions

Along with the dog's eyes, the facial expression is made up of the dog's mouth, teeth, and ears. A dog's entire look can change according to whether the ears are up and forward or down and close to his head. Likewise, the dog would be expressing different emotions.

Here are some different facial expressions to recognize when you see them:

Happy: A happy dog will have a mouth that is relaxed and perhaps slightly open. The teeth will be covered up. The ears might be forward and perked up or they might be down and relaxed.

Alert: An alert dog will have his mouth closed, or it might be slightly open, but the teeth will be covered up. The ears will be up, listening to catch sounds.

Fearful: Fearful dogs have their lips drawn back to show their teeth. Their ears are laid back flat and are kept low on their head.

Aggressive: An aggressive dog will have his lips drawn back in a snarl to show his teeth. He might snap his jaws. His ears might be forward or back, but they will be close to his head.

Submission: The submissive dog's lips will be pulled far back in a "grin" that will show his teeth. Submissive dogs often lick or nuzzle the dog (or person) that scares them. Their ears will be down and flattened against their head.

Play: The playful dog has a mouth that is closed or slightly open. Teeth are covered. The dog might be panting with excitement. Ears might be up and forward or down and relaxed.

Stressed: A stressed dog will have his mouth closed or it might be slightly open in a "grin." The ears are partly back. He might feel indecisive.

The tail

Many people believe they can look at a dog's tail to gauge how the dog is feeling. Unfortunately, this is not always true. Dogs are not quite that easy to read. Sometimes the tail movement does not fit with the rest of the dog's body language. It is important to weigh all of the dog's signals in order to understand what the dog is feeling and how he might act. For instance, an aggressive dog might slowly and stiffly wag his tail  just before he attacks. If you only look at his wagging tail, you might mistakenly think this is a friendly gesture. But, if you look at his lips drawn back and his narrowed eyes, you will not make that mistake.

Here are some signals that dogs send with their tails in various emotional states:

Happy: A happy dog has a tail that is up and out from his body, and he is usually wagging it vigorously. The more interested he is in what is going on, the more vigorously he wags. Some dogs can almost knock you down with their wagging tail.

Alert: An alert dog's tail is typically up, and it might be wagging.

Fearful: A fearful dog keeps his tail between his back legs.

Aggressive: An aggressive dog holds his tail straight out from his body. The hackles on the tail are usually standing up, making the tail look fluffy and big. Sometimes an aggressive dog will slowly, stiffly wag his tail, but this is not a friendly gesture.

Submission: A submissive dog keeps his tail down between his legs.

Play: A dog that is feeling playful wags his tail eagerly. He might give a play bow, bowing in front and holding his tail up over his head as an invitation to play.

Stressed: A stressed dog keeps his tail partly lowered.

You can tell additional information about a dog by the way he wags his tail. A study called "Asymmetric tail-wagging responses by dogs to different emotive stimuli" appeared in the March 20, 2007, issue of *Current Biology* and was reported on in *The New York Times*. In the study, researchers discovered that when dogs have positive feelings about someone or another animal, they wagged their tails to the right side of their bodies. If they had negative feelings, they wagged their tails to the left side of their bodies. According to the scientists, the tail wagging is an indication of which side of the dog's brain is responding to the person or animal. The left brain controls the right side of the body. It is associated with positive feelings such as love, safety, and being calm. The right brain controls the left side of the body. It is associated with fear, depression, and fleeing the scene.

To conduct the tests, the researchers found 30 mixed breed family pets that were taking an agility class. Each dog was placed in a cage with a camera to track the angle of the dog's tail movement. Then the dogs were shown four different kinds of stimuli through an opening in the cage: their owner, an unfamiliar person, a cat, and an unfamiliar, dominant dog. In each case, the dog saw the person or animal for one minute, relaxed for 90 seconds, and then saw the next person or animal.

According to the researchers, the dogs wagged their tails vigorously to the right when they saw their owners. They wagged their tails moderately to the right when they saw an unfamiliar person. Tails wagged slightly to the right when the dogs saw the cat (the cat's owners volunteered him for this experiment). However, when the dogs saw a large, aggressive, unfamiliar dog (a Belgian Malinois), the dogs wagged their tails to the left side of their bodies. According to the researchers, this showed that when the dogs were attracted to something, even an unthreatening cat, they showed positive feelings by wagging their tails to the right; and when they felt negative emotions, they wagged their tails to the left side of their bodies.

You can try this experiment at home with your own dog. Your dog probably always will wag his tail to the right when he sees you. He might wag less enthusiastically if you are trying to get him into the bathtub, however. If he wags his tail to the left at someone or something, take notice.

CASE STUDY: BARBARA AND NASH

Barbara Trice
Romoland, California

Professionally, I have been in dogs for 30 years but have had dogs in my life from day one — that is over 50 years. Currently I have four dogs: three bassets and one Irish setter. At one point, we had a kennel of 17 Irish setters and one beagle.

Paying attention to your dog's body language can be and is very beneficial for their well-being as well as ours. Nine out of ten times, I will guess what they are saying or wanting by the looks that I receive. My Irish will come into the room where I am working on my computer and sometimes just stand and look at me while he wags his tail. This means that he usually needs clean water, or he is looking for a cookie. When he is content, he will walk into the room check me out, walk around once, look out the window, and then go lie down on the couch.

A deep bark means something is approaching the house that he does not understand or he is leery of what is approaching. A rapid bark will alert us that the neighbor cat is walking across the front lawn. And a low deep growl means that the mean neighbor kids are walking by. We have a metal security door that I lock but will usually leave the inside door open. He will sit there and watch the world go by. He has a big dog bed that we place by the door so he is comfortable. On warm days, he will sit there for hours enjoying the birds, cats, and activity.

Usually, I am pretty good at telling what other dogs mean when they bark in the neighborhood. We live on a cul-de-sac, so when the neighbor dogs bark, I have a good idea. At one house, the dogs will fence play, and they bark aggressively. I know what they are doing, but when company comes over, by the barking frightens them because they don't know. Then we have another neighbor that has five large hybrid huskies.

incredibly friendly but have figured out how to get out. They love to come and visit at my house, but the little dogs across the street don't like them being free and bark very rapidly to let the world know that something is array. I will go out front, and they are in my garage looking for a cookie. I get cookies and walk them home and put them back. The only time they bark is when we walk our bassets out of the cul-de-sac.

Years ago, I trained several dogs in obedience and prepared them for dog therapy in hospitals, but I do just the basics now. I have not gone into classes for a long time, but some dogs need more training than others. I am always looking at ways to improve communication with the dogs, but I do that by observing them and trying to figure out what they are trying to tell me.

Some of the everyday words my dogs know are "cookies," "kennel," "home," "outside," and "gopher." My Irish setter is probably one of the smartest dogs I have had in years. When I am returning from work and he is outside looking for gophers or chasing rabbits and he misses the car, my husband will go outside and call to him. He says, "Nash, mommy home," and Nash comes barreling across the acre yard, in through the door, and heads to my bedroom or the computer room. He is wagging his tail to beat the band. He also is the one that when you say, "kennel," he will open the kennel door and lie down until he gets his cookie.

My Irish setter Kelsey (whom I lost recently) was perfect at communicating with me. Her favorite spot was on the corner of the couch or by the front door. When something was wrong, she always would come and get me. She had very hard nails, and we have wood floors, so when she needed me, she knew to come and tap dance with her nails and gently woo woo until I got up. One night at about 2 a.m., she came to my bedside and tapped danced to wake me up. I discovered that the field behind our house had caught on fire. She immediately knew it was wrong and got us. She would do the same thing when she would get sick. She would come and tell me if we were sleeping. Over the 14 years of her life, she would get our attention with her tap dancing, and no one ever disregarded her when she would tap dance. Many times she would do that to tell us she needed fresh water outside, by standing by the bucket waiting for you to dump out the old water and fill it with fresh. She would go outside and find her soft squeeze toy, the only one that she would look for. She would go to all her favorite hiding spots until she found it, then she would bring it to our feet and bark, telling us to pick it up and throw it. She would go and pounce on it, throw it around, and then do it again repeatedly until she was done. Then she would go and hide it again, get a drink, and lie under the shade tree.

My Irish has a sensitive tummy. When he is not feeling up to par, he lets me know by hesitating to go into his kennel. Usually my dogs are not kenneled except for their dinner times (so I know what they eat and how much), so if they don't eat, I know something is wrong. So when he hesitates, I know he is not feeling well or he senses something is wrong outside.

My one male basset is good at alerting us if someone is in the garage. He will stand quietly at the garage door and listen, then he runs to us and back to the door to tell us someone is here. He has never been wrong.

I personally try hard to understand their barks, their head twists, or ears or woo woos. If you listen and pay attention, you usually will figure it out. Many years ago, my dog Smokey (my heart dog) and I did therapy work in the local hospitals and schools. So many times, he could sense when a person was going to die or go into a coma because he would not want to leave them until he was ready. For people who did not show emotions, he would nudge their hands until they would pet his head, and usually a short time later they would begin to cry, expressing their loss of a loved pet or a family member. He had an incredible talent when he was around children and elderly people. He was a miracle dog, and very communicative. When he was showing in the ring, I knew he did not like it, so when we would go, I would ask him to do his best and he did. When he completed his title we stopped, then began obedience and therapy. He would bound to the door when it was time to go, telling me that now it was his time to do what he wanted to do and for me to do my best.

My Irish does have behavior problems that might be due to miscommunication. He likes to bark at me when it is not necessary. I'm sure he has received miscommunication from me at some point, and I have not figured out how to fix it. He will bark sometimes when I talk to him, so either he is sassing me back or having fun mimicking me. He wags his tail when he does this, so I figure he is laughing at me. Sometimes I have to hold him by his collar and tell him to stop before he does. I'm certain that it is my fault that he started this, so I have no one to blame but me.

I have been ill recently, and all of them know that. They were gentle when I returned home from the hospital and were all interested in lying on the bed with me when I was recovering. They were mindful not to get on top of me so not to hurt me and were very attentive when I was up and walking around. Many times at night when I couldn't sleep any longer, I would go to the computer and work, and they were all right there curled up by my feet. Also, on the night that I had a gallbladder attack, my Irish began barking nonstop to wake up the house because it was not normal to him, and he was uncomfortable that I was not acting right. So, I am pretty glad that they understand that something is wrong.

I would highly suggest that owners just spent some time with their dogs. They will tell you when they are nervous by their tails and when they are happy. Their eyes will tell you that they don't feel good or they don't want you to go, or that they want you to play ball with them. They will alert you to danger and will protect you. Dogs are used as Seeing Eye® dogs for a reason, because they can sense good, bad and evil. Many dogs are trained to do so many things, but if you let your dog be himself, and you treat him with respect and love, the dogs will always, always return that favor. They love us unconditionally and will give back if allowed too. Spend the day with your dogs often, and they will teach you (us) what they need, want and enjoy. They are incredibly smart animals.

Vocalization

Vocalization is one of the differences between wolves and dogs. Adult wolves rarely bark, while adult dogs sometimes bark too much. Some researchers have theorized that this barking-vocalization is something that humans selected during domestication of the dog. Vocalization is more of a trait found in wolf cubs in the wild, and humans might have found it to be useful. Perhaps dogs that could bark and

give a warning in the village were valued. Or, perhaps they valued dogs that could bark or bay during hunting to indicate where the prey was to be found. Whatever the case, modern dogs vocalize much more than their wolf relatives. We picture the lonely wolf howling at the moon, but we are more likely to hear our neighbors' dogs barking in the distance.

On the other hand, dogs do not rely on barking as their primary means of communication. Body language is much more important to your dog than barking or the other sounds that dogs make. Puppies are born with their eyes sealed shut and their ears closed. They cannot see until they are at least 2 weeks old, and they do not start to hear until they are about 3 weeks old. They do make a number of whimpering and crying sounds in these early weeks so their mother can find them if they move away from the nest. They let their mother know if they are too cold or too hot or if they are hungry. But puppies do not begin to make little barks until they are about 3 weeks old when they can start to hear and see things. Puppies almost seem to surprise themselves when they first make little barks; they seem unaware that they can make that sound. They sometimes fall over when they bark at that age, perhaps because they put so much force into each little bark.

As they get older, dogs bark for many different reasons:

- 🐾 Dogs bark to give a warning or alert. ("There's a squirrel in the yard!" Or, "The garbage truck is taking our stuff!" Or, "The house is on fire!")

- 🐾 Dogs bark because they are lonely or anxious. ("Why did you leave me here all alone?")

- 🐾 Dogs bark to identify themselves or their location. ("I'm here!")

- 🐾 Dogs bark when they play. ("This is *fun!*" "Run, run, *run!*" or "Tag! You're it!")

- 🐾 Dogs bark to get attention. ("Pet me, pet me, pet me, *pet me, please!*" "Feed me," or *"Feed me!"* "I want to come inside.")

- 🐾 Dogs bark when they are bored. ("Bark, bark, barkbarkbark, I'm bored, bark barkbark.")

- 🐾 Dogs bark when they are startled. ("Hey, you scared me!")

- 🐾 Dogs bark when they are frustrated. ("I hate that cat sitting on the other side of the fence!")

These are common occasions that will elicit barks from your dog. Some will result in your dog giving just one or two barks. Others will result in your dog barking for a long time.

When you first hear a dog barking, all barks might sound alike, but if you listen closely, you can learn to distinguish between barks. Dogs have dozens of different kinds of barks, from happy and playful to frustrated and sad. They express all kinds of emotion with their barking.

Evidence suggests humans are good at understanding what a dog means when he barks, even if they cannot see the dog to read his body language. In 2005, a researcher in Hungary published findings in *The Journal of Comparative Psychology* (Vol. 119, No. 2) that showed humans could understand whether dogs in an audio recording were being aggressive, fearful, or playful. According to the researcher, the findings suggested that barking was an important part of the canine-human relationship.

The study used a Hungarian dog breed called Mudis for the research. Dogs were taped in six barking situations: when a stranger came to the door of the dog owner's house; when a trainer pretended to be a "bad guy" and encouraged the dog to bark aggressively and bite padding on his arm; when the dog's owner took a leash and got ready to take the dog for a walk; when the dog was taken to a park and was left alone, tied to a tree; when the owner played a tug of war game with the dog; and when the owner held a favorite toy or ball a few feet away from the dog.

The researcher then played the recordings of the dogs barking for 36 people who were part of the study. Twelve of the people were Mudi owners; 12 people owned other dog breeds; and 12 people did not own a dog at all. All the participants were able to correctly categorize the aggressive, playful, or fearful emotions of the dogs' barks far above chance. There were no significant differences between the abilities of  the Mudi owners and the other owners and non-dog owners. The findings suggested that humans are able to understand dog barks when they hear them. A follow up study in 2011 with children ages 6, 8, and 10 found that understanding dog barks seems to be innate with children and with humans. According to the study, preadolescents might have a natural talent for understanding dog barks.

You are probably good at understanding your dog's barks whether you realize it or not. Some breeds tend to bark more than others. Hound breeds are somewhat notorious for barking, especially scent hounds, but this is due to their original purpose. Many of these breeds were bred to give voice when they found the scent of their prey, so hunters could follow them. Today this trait is often less desirable, especially if you live in an apartment or the suburbs. Shetland sheepdogs are another breed known for barking. Some toy breeds also bark a great deal. In some cases, you can train dogs to curtail the excess barking. *This will be discussed in Chapter 7.* Other breeds do not bark much or any. The basenji is known as "the barkless dog." This does not mean they are silent; basenjis produce a yodeling sound.

You would not want to stop your dog from barking completely. Barking is a normal means of communication. Sometimes your dog is giving you important information when he barks. ("Hey, someone is breaking into the house!") It is only when dogs engage in nuisance barking that it becomes a problem.

In addition to barking, dogs make some other sounds you should recognize:

The Howl: A dog usually howls because he is lost or looking for someone, perhaps you. Your dog might howl when you go to work, for example. A dog or wolf separated from his pack will howl so he can locate them or they can find him. When one dog howls, it normally gets a response from other dogs. "Here I am."

The Growl: A growl is a warning to back off, whether it is directed at another dog or you. Depending on the dog's posture, you will know if he is being aggressive or bluffing. A dog that has his eyes narrowed and his teeth bared should be taken seriously.

The Grunt or Mutter: The grunt or mutter can almost sound like a "grrrr" growl with some dogs. It is not a threat; it is a complaint. Your dog knows he will get in trouble if he barks or demands something, but he wants something and this is a slightly more polite way of asking for it.

The Whimper: A dog will whimper if he is hurt or anxious. This is typically a sound that a puppy makes. Some adult dogs whimper to get attention.

The Whine: A whining dog is frustrated and complaining.

Calming Signals

Dogs also give what are called "calming signals," dog-to-dog and dog-to-human. Calming signals are specific kinds of body movements and signals that your dog uses to avoid or resolve conflict situations. Your dog uses these signals to avoid threats, calm down a tense situation, reduce fear and nervousness in himself and in another dog, avoid something unpleasant, make things safer, or signal that he does not want to fight.

Author Turid Rugaas is known for her work on calming signals. She has written a book called, *On Talking Terms With Dogs: Calming Signals in Dogs*.

She writes, "Wolves and dogs try to avoid conflict, they are conflict-solving animals. It is usually US, the human species, who make conflicts between our dogs and us." You could accidentally cause a conflict with your dog in many situations, so you should be able to read your dog's calming signals. For example, if your dog comes over to you and noses around, you might command him to "sit." Your commanding tone might cause your dog to yawn (a calming signal) before he sits down. When you put the leash on your dog, he pulls slightly, and you jerk the leash. Your dog turns his back to you (a calming signal) and lowers his nose to the ground (another calming signal).

Examples such as these happen all the time in our daily communication with dogs, but we rarely notice the signals our dogs are giving us to calm down. Your dog is telling you he wishes to avoid confrontation.

Author Experiences: Peyton

Peyton (her litter was born during the AFC playoffs) is one of my other show dogs, and she is Pearl's daughter (you were introduced to Pearl in the introduction). She seems to have inherited Pearl's gift for communication. She is vocal and makes grring sounds when she wants something. She will bark at me when I speak to her. She likes to place a paw on my leg when I am working to get my attention and tell me she wants something. But aside from her "verbal" gifts, Peyton has a unique quality that makes her invaluable in my home. She is the greatest peacemaker I have ever known. If you have multiple dogs, then there are bound to be times when tensions are high and dogs do not get along. Someone takes someone's favorite sleeping place. Someone looks at someone funny. Someone is simply having a bad day. For these occasions, I have Peyton. Since she was a tiny puppy, Peyton has thrown herself wholeheartedly into these scenes. She will get between two unhappy dogs, kiss faces, lay on her back, wag her tail, and make nice with both dogs until they are happy again. I seldom have any ill feelings or squabbles at my house since Peyton was born, and I think it is because of her wonderful skills as a diplomat. I have watched her carefully and learned a great deal about the calming signals she uses to defuse tension. All dogs know these calming signals, but few dogs can use them as well as Peyton.

Many times the signals come in multiples and they might be given quickly. But with patience and some experience, you can learn to read them. Here are some typical calming signals used by dogs:

Your dog turns his head away. This signal is often given quickly. Sometimes the dog darts his eyes away or from side to side. The dog might turn his head to the side and keep it there.

Your dog turns away. Your dog turns away from you or turns his back to you. This is calming for him. You might see this if your dog is playing with another dog that starts playing too wildly. In some cases, a dog will turn away from a dog that is threatening him.

Your dog licks his nose. This often occurs so quickly that most people do not see it happen. If your dog is nervous, he might lick his nose. Dogs will sometimes do this if they are approaching another dog.

Your dog yawns. You might think it is funny or cute when your dog yawns, but in reality, dogs usually yawn when they are anxious or trying to reduce tension. (Though sometimes a yawn is just a yawn.) Your dog might yawn when you take him someplace where he feels stressed, such as the vet's office. He might yawn if he is in a situation that makes him feel uncomfortable, such as being squeezed by a child,  for instance. You can yawn at your dog to help him reduce stress and relax.

Your dog "shakes off." This is a behavior often seen in dogs. It is not the same "shaking off" a dog does following a bath. It is like a reset. For instance, if two dogs have been playing wildly and one accidentally gets hurt, you will see the dogs "shake off." They might separate for a minute, collect themselves, and decide if they want to continue to play.

By learning to recognize these calming signals, you can improve communication with your dog and avoid unnecessary conflicts. Your dog does not want to be in conflict with you. Chances are that he often gives you signals that he wants to avoid problems. Learn these signals, and your relationship should go more smoothly.

In some cases, you can mimic your dog's calming signals when he displays them to let him know that you are receiving them and that you, too, wish to avoid conflict. For example, if you are grooming your dog and he turns his head away from you because he does not like what you are doing, you also can turn your head away momentarily. You can ease up on what you are doing that is causing your dog distress, such as trimming his nails. Grooming is stressful for some dogs, though other dogs enjoy it. Giving and receiving the calming signals can be a way of negotiating with your dog to show him that you are mindful of what he is telling you, and you are trying to be sensitive to it.

In another possible scenario, you might take your dog to the vet's office, which could cause him to feel stressed. He might lick his nose quickly because he is nervous. It is not likely that you can lick your nose to reassure him, but you can pet him to help calm him and speak soothingly to him. Sometimes just being able to read your dog's signals is helpful.

Breed Differences

If you are only familiar
with one breed of dog,
you might not consider
how different breeds
communicate, but
different breeds can have
physical and mental
differences that cause

them to communicate in slightly different ways. Temperament
can vary enormously among breeds, which can also lead to dogs
expressing themselves differently in the same circumstances.
Just the fact that dogs have ears that are shaped differently,
such as prick ears, long ears, rosebud ears, and ears of other
shapes, means you cannot always look at the ears to see how
a dog is feeling. The same is true of the dog's tail. Many dogs
have long tails, but other dogs have docked tails, and some
dogs have naturally bobbed tails. It is hard to tell if a tail is
wagging when it is absent.

Mental and temperamental differences between breeds
mean that if you have a Labrador retriever and a German
shepherd — both popular breeds — these two dogs will react
quite differently to nearly everything. They will have different
impulses with regard to approaching strangers, socialization,
and training. These breeds are both extremely intelligent,
and you can enjoy great communication with each of them,
but your approach to working with the two dogs would be

different. Keep these facts in mind as you work with your dog and remember to adapt information about socialization and training to fit your dog.

Males and Females

Most experienced dog people seem to believe there are temperament differences between male and female dogs. Male dogs are generally perceived as being sweeter and more affectionate toward their owners, while female dogs are thought to be tougher and more independent. In the home, when males and females live together, female dogs often rule. This is not to say that female dogs are less loving or devoted to their owners, or that male dogs cannot be tough. But male dogs are seen as *more* affectionate and female dogs are seen as *more* independent. These differences can affect how you communicate with your dog and train. Your male dog could be more eager to please you, for example; while you might have to convince your female dog that it is worth her while or in her best interest to do as you say. With that said, female dogs are sometimes thought to be more intelligent, or to learn faster than male dogs. This is often true with housetraining, for example. Developmentally, female puppies are usually ahead of their male counterparts in the whelping box for the first few weeks; they do things first and learn faster, even when male puppies are larger.

When male and female dogs are altered, they can experience personality changes. Some owners who work with performance dogs (dogs competing in events such as field trials and other

sports) prefer not to spay or neuter their dogs because they feel the dogs lose a competitive edge. Studies suggest that female dogs might become more aggressive toward other dogs when spayed, though this is not guaranteed to happen. Some female dogs might only become a little cranky after spaying; and some female dogs might not exhibit any personality changes. Male dogs can become mellower after being neutered, though again this is only a general observation from owners. In many cases, altering both males and females can lower their metabolism because of the absence of the sexual hormones and make them more susceptible to gaining weight. If you spay or neuter your dog, you will need to pay close attention to how much you feed your dog and make sure he continues to get plenty of regular exercise.

On the other hand, if you have an intact male dog, he can be distracted during training at times by the presence of a female dog in heat. Female dogs will come in heat once or twice a year, usually, so having an intact female can interfere with your training if you are doing serious daily training for an event. Your girl might not be as interested in training at this time. Different girls behave differently when they are in season.

Some events, such as field trials, will not allow a female dog in heat to compete because they would be a distraction to the other dogs, so if your girl comes in season after you have entered the event, you will lose your entry money. Many dog sports require dogs to be intact, however, such as conformation dog shows, because dogs are being evaluated as breeding stock. Female dogs in heat can be shown, though exhibitors sometimes keep their girls home if they come in season as a courtesy. Other exhibitors show their female dogs anyway (though the handler should advise the judge before he or she examines the girl). Male dogs just have to learn to behave well when they are around girls in heat. A female dog in heat is considered just another element of the show they have to learn to contend with, like spectators and judges. The handler should work with the male dog and train him appropriately ahead of time. Many young male dogs still become googly-eyed and do not perform well when a girl in heat is being shown with them, but more experienced males usually handle the situation better.

For a full discussion of the pros and cons of spaying and neutering, you can visit the American College of Theriogenology website: **www.theriogenology.org**. Theriogenologists are veterinarians who specialize in reproduction. You can also read *Long-Term Health Effects of Spay Neuter In Dogs* by Laura J. Sanborn, which discusses the age at which to spay or neuter your dog at **www.naiaonline.org/pdfs/ LongTermHealthEffectsOfSpayNeuterInDogs.pdf**. The best age to spay or neuter your dog can depend on many factors including your dog's breed and gender.

If you are trying to decide whether a male or female dog would make a better pet for you, they both have their advantages. It is really a matter of personal preference. The most important thing is the dog's individual personality and how the two of you get along.

Your Dog's Senses

Many times dogs seem to understand us or "read" us so quickly and easily that it almost seems like they must be telepathic. How else can we explain dogs that seem to know what we are doing even when they are in another room or dogs waiting by the door when we come home from work? In fact, studies have been done about dogs and ESP. *There will be more on this subject in Chapter 2.*

For the most part, dogs use the same senses humans have, though they use some of them much more effectively than we do. The dog's sense of smell is legendary. In fact, the dog has up to 220 million smell receptors. The average dog can have a sense of smell that is between 100,000 and 1 million times more sensitive than the human sense of smell. Some dogs, such as bloodhounds, can have noses that are even more sensitive.

Dogs also have a range of hearing that is much higher than the human range. They can hear things beyond our upper limit. Dogs are able to flex and rotate their ears, which allow them to pinpoint the source of a sound. Dogs are also able to hear sounds from four times farther away than humans can.

Contrary to popular belief, dogs do not see the world in black and white or shades of gray. They do see colors. They are red-green color-blind and cannot tell the difference between these two colors, but they can see other colors. They also see fewer shades of gray than humans do. They are considered dichromatic, as most mammals are. Humans are trichromatic, which means we see three primary colors. Although a dog's sharpness of vision or visual acuity is not good compared to a human's, they are good at perceiving moving objects, and dogs are good at seeing in dim light, both traits that help them as hunters.

Our dogs can use their senses to observe us by paying attention to our facial expressions, our voices, the way we move, our body odor, our interactions with other humans, and countless other things we never stop to think about during the day. Your dog probably knows you better than anyone. He knows what you ate for dinner, when you went to the bathroom, how often you do laundry, who your friends are, and what your mood is. He knows if you like the movie you are watching. He knows you.

You know your dog, too, though you might not stop to think about how he carries his ears or his facial expressions or what each individual bark means. You take in this information and understand it. The next chapter will look at the ways we communicate with our dogs and how we use our own body language and other means to exchange information with them. Dogs are often so much a part of our lives that we do not think about how we communicate with them, but our methods are just as complex as those used by our canine friends.

CHAPTER TWO

Ways We Communicate with Our Dogs

Dogs and humans probably are able to communicate so well because we are both social species. Communication is important for both of us. Humans are great communicators. We not only talk, use our hands, and give facial expressions as well as body language, but we also have created reading and writing, computers, phones, and so many other kinds of communication technology. Humans are all about communication. Dogs might not be able to read and write or use Twitter®, but they do not really need to do so to understand us. Your dog can understand you just from the tone of your voice.

Verbal Communication

Verbal communication is not nearly as important to dogs as it is to humans, but humans rely on it to a considerable extent when communicating with their dogs. Most people talk to their dogs regularly. Being able to confide in a dog is one of the pleasures of owning a dog; they make wonderful listeners. Although it is true that dogs do not seem to understand

verbal syntax or sentences, they do learn words. You might tell your dog something, and he will look at you with a slightly confused faced until you say some word that he recognizes, and then all will become clear for him. That is all he needs to know to understand what you are saying. We might sound like Charlie Brown's teacher to our dogs: all noise until they hear the key word they understand.

Dogs also seem to understand us according to our tone of voice. It is standard practice among dog trainers to tell their students to use a positive, upbeat tone of voice, a "happy" voice, when training their dogs. Dogs respond much better to training when you use this happy voice, which might be much higher and more cheerful than your ordinary voice. This goes along with making training fun. The more you can make training like a game, the easier most dogs will learn.

Of course, it is not always possible to use the happy tone of voice at home, 24/7. Dogs can also tell when you are being fake, and no one is happy all the time. Your dog can tell your mood by your tone of voice, no matter how you feel.

Despite the fact that verbal communication is not the best way for dogs to understand us, some dogs excel at it. Rico, born in 1994, first came to the attention of scientists at the Max Planck Institute for Evolutionary Anthropology in Leipzig, Germany, when he appeared on a German variety show. Rico amazed viewers by fetching his toys and stuffed animals by name. Your dog can probably do this, too, but Rico's owners said that Rico had a vocabulary of more than 200 words. Rico's owners started training him to learn the names of toys when he was sick at 10 months old and could not leave the house. The scientists were intrigued but skeptical. They asked Rico's owners if they could test the 9-year-old dog's learning abilities.

To give you some context, Koko the gorilla has a working vocabulary of more than 1,000 signs and understands about 2,000 words of spoken English. She has been learning language skills for more than 30 years.

In order to proceed, the scientists needed to find out if Rico's ability was due to the "Clever Hans Effect." Clever Hans was a famous horse at the turn of the 20th century that also happened to entertain the German public. Like Rico, he seemed to have almost human intelligence. He solved math and calculus problems and answered all manner of questions by stomping his hoof on the ground to count or to indicate "yes" or "no." He even was advertised as the "smartest animal in the world." But it all went wrong when a knowledgeable psychologist devised a series of experiments that revealed Hans was receiving (possibly) unintentional cues from his trainer. If the trainer did not know the answer or was out of the horse's sight, Hans had no way to receive those subtle cues and could not answer. He did not know when to stop counting or when to indicate the number of stomps for "yes" or "no."

The scientists working with Rico designed a series of experiments to test him. They placed ten of Rico's 200 familiar toys (apparently, Rico had 200 toys) in a separate room. In each separate trial, Rico's owner told him to fetch a specific toy by name. Rico would then go into the separate room where he could not see either his owner or the scientists. There were no visual cues to influence him. During these tests, Rico successfully brought back the correct toy 37 out of 40 times. That is a 92.5 percent success rate for bringing back the correct toy by name. That seemed to thoroughly put to rest any worry about the "Clever Hans Effect." Rico really knew the names of his toys. His vocabulary was comparable to dolphins, apes, sea lions, and parrots that have undergone extensive training.

The scientists also wanted to test Rico for something called "fast mapping." Fast mapping is a learning strategy that partially characterizes vocabulary acquisition during early childhood. Young children begin a process of rapid vocabulary acquisition around 2 years old, and it peaks between ages 6 to 10 when children learn as many as ten new words per day.

Learning by fast mapping indicates that children innately know new words and tend to refer to objects that do not already have names. It allows children to learn new words quickly usually on the first attempt, based on limited exposure to the words, and to remember them later. The scientists wanted to find out if humans were the only ones with this ability, or if Rico could do it, too.

"Fast mapping was thought to be something exclusively human. It is how children learn the meanings of new words," study author Julia Fischer said. "Nobody thought this could be done by an animal."

To test Rico's fast mapping abilities, the researchers placed eight toys in the room next door. Rico already knew the names for seven of the toys, but he had never seen one of the toys before. After one or two successful attempts at fetching the familiar toys, Rico was told to bring back the new toy, referred to with a new word.

To test Rico, the researchers made up unusual, nonsensical words for the new toys. "Sirikid" was a blue, stuffed toy dragon, and "siebenstern" was a stuffed raven. There was no way that Rico could know the words, and he had not heard them previously, even in a context other than naming his toys.

On his first try, Rico correctly retrieved the new toy. In the following trials, Rico was right seven out of ten times.

The trials also succeeded in testing something called "exclusionary learning." Rico's ability to understand the name of an unfamiliar object among a cluster of familiar ones demonstrated "exclusionary learning," another human learning ability that had not been expected in dogs.

"This tells us he can do simple logic," Fischer said. "It's like he's saying to himself, 'I know the others have names so this word cannot refer to my familiar toys. It must refer to this new thing.' Or it goes the other way around, and he is thinking, 'I've never seen this one before, so this must be it.' He is actually thinking."

Still not satisfied, the scientists wanted to know if, like human children, Rico would remember the words he had learned through fast mapping. Four weeks later, they went back to Rico's house to do a final test. This time they placed nine objects in the next room: four were Rico's familiar toys, four were toys he had never seen before, and one was a toy he had retrieved during the fast mapping test a month earlier. After a couple of warm-up tests with familiar toys, Rico was asked to fetch the toy he had learned by fast mapping. He brought out the correct toy. He got it right three out of six times, a rate comparable to what a typical 3-year-old human toddler could do.

"Of course, for a child, a word very rapidly means much more than it does for a dog. They will quickly know it is a color word or an activity word. Their representation will be much richer than it is for a dog," Fischer said. "But in terms of this task, he is as smart as kids are."

Is Rico as smart as a child? No. Rico's fast mapping ability puts him on a par with a toddler, but the sheer number of words that a child knows aside, Rico's vocabulary is largely focused on toys and food, while a child is able to gradually grasp more complex concepts and feelings. However, Rico's learning process certainly shows that dogs and humans have more in common than many people once thought.

"We know now that the dog rapidly can associate new words with new objects, which is just what children do right at the point that language takes off," said Sue Savage-Rumbaugh, a former Georgia State University researcher who now works for the Great Apes Project. "So the dog is on the border of very complex language ability."

Fischer explained that Rico's demonstrated ability to learn by fast mapping "shows that fast mapping is not specific to humans, that it probably has a more general purpose in figuring things out in your world."

Is it also possible that Rico is exceptional? Do we have any way of knowing how representative he is of other dogs? He could be, as one researcher suggested, the Albert Einstein of dogs, or is he just a typical dog in terms of his vocabulary and ability to learn? Does the fact that he is a border collie — a breed generally recognized as being intelligent — plays a role in his abilities? There is no way to know without working with many more dogs in similar tests.

Harvard psychologist Susan Carey, whose Laboratory for Developmental Studies investigates how infants and young children reason about the world around them, said the research with Rico is both significant and scientifically important.

"The evidence that it can exhibit what we call 'exclusionary learning' and 'fast mapping' is the most spectacular finding in the report," Carey said. "That any dog can do it at all is really, really surprising, even though merely associating words and objects has long been known among other researchers studying animals as varied as apes, seals, dolphins, and parrots.

"I'm convinced that this dog has the abilities claimed for it, but is it really understanding true communication beyond merely learning to obey commands?" Carey questioned. "Dogs are adapted by evolution and breeding to communicate with humans, but is this one actually communicating with reason and really learning language the way human children do? We need to know a lot more to answer that question."

"A lot of people have argued that the perceptual and cognitive mechanism that underlie what we call language and speech acquisition are unique to humans," said Mark Bekoff, who studies dogs at the University of Colorado. "What this study shows clearly is that is not the case. What this shows is that other animals possess those cognitive and perceptual abilities."

Fischer said, "Rico is clearly capable of independent thinking and using simple logic. Of course, a child has a much richer and broader understanding of words than a dog or any other animal. But with all the other claims we're receiving from other owners, we'll have the chance for much more research into this question."

"Rico is a very smart listener," Fischer said. "He just doesn't say much."

Katrina Kelner, *Science*'s deputy editor for life sciences, sums it up: "Such fast, one-trial learning in dogs is remarkable. This ability suggests that the brain structures that support this kind of learning are not unique to humans, and may have formed the evolutionary basis of some of the advanced language abilities of humans."

We still do not know how or why language developed in humans. We do not know which aspects of human language are unique to humans and which are present in other species. Our communication with our dogs can, oddly enough, help us learn about ourselves, as Rico has shown. However, what these tests did not measure, but what dog-lovers already know, is that dogs also have emotional intelligence that allows them to empathize with us and choose to be our companions. They pass those tests with flying colors every day.

In the past few years, several other dogs have been discovered that also have phenomenal language abilities similar to Rico's. At least two of these dogs have vocabularies of more than 1,000 words. Clearly, some, if not all, dogs have the ability to understand verbal communication with us, and their thinking abilities might be beyond what anyone expected.

CASE STUDY: KRYS AND HER BORDER COLLIES

Krys Brennand
Le Sueur, Minnesota

I have had dogs nearly 50 years. We currently have four dogs: three border collies and one fox terrier.

I am usually aware of my dogs' body language; for some things, the body language would be the same but in some instances an individual dog will behave in a way dependent upon his character. The ears and tail seem particularly expressive, also the position of the head and movement of the body.

I very often can tell what the dogs want when they look at me, especially the border collies. Very often, they will look at me and then look toward what they want or what they want me to do. For instance, if they want me to play, they will look at me and then look at the toy; if that doesn't work, they will position the toy a bit closer in a place I could not fail to notice.

If they want to go out, or maybe just have me open the door, one of the border collies will tap her paw onto the glass (her nails make a tinkling sound). If I do not hear, she will give a short yip to get my attention. The same border collie will push a toy at my hand as I am walking, place the toy in my lap if I am sitting, or place the toy in the dishwasher if I am loading/unloading. One of the other border collies leans heavily into me when he wants attention. The terrier sits patiently by a door for it to open.

To some extent, I can ascertain different meanings from their barks. There is the frantic loud barking that means a car is driving up our lane or someone is coming to the door. There is the yip type, "notice me" type bark. There's the "let me out — something is bothering the chickens" (even if the alarmed chickens happen to be on TV) bark. There is the sharp, rapid barking one of the border collies does when there is something new she thinks might be threatening.

The border collies know more words than I am aware of them knowing. It is a bit hard to tell with the terrier, as she is less biddable than the border collies. Our terrier knows her name, "dinner," "sit" (for a treat), "in," "out," "come," and probably other words; she responds pretty well to food treats as incentive but she is less likely to respond without incentive, especially if she would prefer to do something else. A couple of the border collies know the names of several toys, items of human clothing, names of the humans and other animals in the house, various commands, more or less any word we wish to teach. They have also picked up many untaught words.

One needs to be consistent in communicating with dogs. I think it is important the dog is not physically punished for unwanted behavior; a firmly spoken "no" if one catches the dog in the act of unwanted behavior usually seems to suffice. Rewarding desirable behavior seems to help learning, so praise when they get it right. With some dogs, food treats seem to work very well; with others, play, even if only throwing a toy once, works well.

Sometimes fear provokes an undesirable response. I find patience and not forcing the issue helps.

Touch

Petting your dog is one of the surest and most direct ways of communicating with him. The sense of touch is the first sense developed in newborn puppies. They can tell the difference between  warm and cold places in the nest, and they seek out the touch of their mother for comfort, in addition to nursing. Touching and tumbling with their littermates even before their eyes open help to stimulate growth and encourages nursing. Dogs use the sense of touch to communicate with other dogs and with humans. You often will see dogs touching noses with each other, pawing at another dog, giving a doggy friend a good-natured swat, or poking their owner to be petted.

Dogs seem to benefit from the touch that comes with petting as much as humans do. In humans, petting a dog has been shown to lower blood pressure and reduce the heart rate, among other health benefits. Likewise, petting reduces blood pressure and heart rate in dogs.

Dogs also use their sense of touch to investigate the world around them. The muzzle is sensitive to touch, and the whiskers (vibrissae) contain sensory nerves at their base that can tell the dog about the things he is feeling with them. They let the dog know about things in relation to his head.

Dogs are particularly sensitive on their muzzles and the back of their necks, known as the "scruff." These are the areas where a mother dog will discipline a young puppy. When touching a dog, you might find that he is cautious about having these places touched. Most dogs do not like to have their heads patted either. It is usually best to approach a dog for petting with your hand lowered and to pet him under the throat or on the side of the neck instead of patting him on the head.

Some male dogs are ticklish about having their genitals touched if you are bathing them. Other dogs do not like to have their ears investigated or cleaned, though this is usually because the dog has had a bad ear-cleaning experience. Likewise, some dogs are foot shy, or they do not like to have someone bothering their paws. This is often because they have had a bad experience with someone trimming their nails. However, in some cases, dogs do not like to have their paws held or examined because they have a more assertive/independent personality.

You can use some forms of touch on your dog that are soothing. Massage therapy, for example, can be beneficial for your dog as long as you do not use deep massage without proper training.

TTouch™, or the Tellington Touch™, is a specialized approach to care and training for animals, not just dogs. With this method, you use circular movements of your fingers and hands all over the animal's body. The creators of this method say that it is like "turning on the electric lights of the body." Practitioners say that you do not have to understand anatomy to be successful with using TTouch and that it will speed up the healing of ailments and injuries and even change an animal's undesirable behavior and habits.

For most people, just spending time petting your dog is a good way to improve communication. It will make your dog happy and make you feel better. Some dogs enjoy petting more than others. But nearly all dogs enjoy some degree of touch and petting.

Body Language

Your dog reads your body language as easily as he reads the body language of another dog. When you have your head held high, your dog rightly assumes that you are feeling good and have a good opinion of yourself. When your head is lowered in thought, your dog knows something is wrong. He can read your body language to know if you are sad or depressed. He can look at the body language of strangers and see what it is communicating about

them. The man strutting down the street is as obvious to your dog as he is to you. The person shuffling along, hunched over, and feeling down, stands out to your dog, too, as does everyone else your dog sees. He is good at sizing people up based on how they present themselves. He might not always be right, but he is probably as good as humans are at reading body language, or maybe better.

One of the most important ways dogs read us, especially our own dogs, is by reading our facial expressions and watching our eyes. Several similar studies have been done that have proved dogs focus on our eyes and expressions in order to know what we are thinking or what we are going to do. In one study, dogs were shown to study tiny details and correctly interpret human intentions. The study was published in the journal, *Current Biology*. Dogs were presented with two videos. In the first video, a woman says, "Hi, dog," and looks straight at the camera. Then she turns her head and looks at a container. The dog also follows her gaze and looks at the container. In the second video, the woman says, "Hi, dog," but she is looking down. When she then looks at the container, the dog does not follow her gaze.

According to the researchers, the study shows dogs can pick up on subtle human behavior, such as when they are being spoken to. It would also seem to suggest that the dogs could follow the woman's glance when they were looking at her eyes. Human infants have been shown to have this same ability. One of the co-authors of the study said that dogs are receptive to human communication in a manner that was previously attributed only to humans. Canine behavior expert Stanley Coren believes that in terms of development, dogs are on the same level as 2-year-olds.

Dr. Coren in *Modern Dog Magazine*'s "How Dogs Read Body Language" reports on another series of experiments. Discussing social cognition and how dogs understand social cues, Dr. Coren describes a test with upside down buckets. Under one of the buckets, the researchers placed some food. Both buckets were rubbed with the food, so they smelled the same. The researcher would indicate which bucket contained the food by touching it, pointing at it, nodding toward it, or glancing at it. If the subject chooses the right bucket, they would get the food. The test was conducted with chimpanzees, 3-year-old children, dogs, wolves, and 9-week-old puppies.

To the surprise of the researchers, the dogs outperformed everyone in following the social cues and choosing the correct bucket that contained the food. They were four times better than the chimps and twice as good as the children. The wolves were not as good as the chimps and much worse than the dogs.

Puppies were tested to find out if the dogs were able to read the social cues because they were knowledgeable about living with humans and reading body language. But 9-week-old puppies, still living with their mother and not yet pets, were still good at choosing the right buckets. Dogs have an exceptional ability to read human body language and social cues, and they have it from the time they are puppies. It is not something they have to learn, though living with people undoubtedly sharpens their communication skills.

Coren goes on to theorize about the implications of this study. Did early humans choose dogs that were better at reading human body language and understanding us? Or, is the ability to read  human body language a secondary part of domestication? Did it occur as a byproduct of the other changes that humans selected for when they were choosing dogs that were tamer and less aggressive? We have no way of knowing now.

At any rate, dogs easily can read your glances and facial expressions. If you look toward your dog's leash, he is probably on his way to the door. If your eyes flicker to his food bowl, your dog will be up and wagging his tail, telling you it is time to feed him. Sometimes these actions can seem almost telepathic, but there is good reason to think that your dog is picking up on the subtle clues you are giving, perhaps without even realizing it.

Can Dogs Read Minds?

Dogs are so good at reading us, you might have wondered sometimes if they have ESP. Rupert Sheldrake (www.sheldrake.org), in Britain, has done a great deal of research into animal telepathy, especially involving dogs. You might know him as the man who wrote the books *Seven Experiments That Could Change The World* (1995), *Dogs That Know When Their Owners Are Coming Home* (1999), and *The Sense of Being Stared At* (2003).

Dr. Sheldrake, who has degrees from Cambridge and Harvard, is a biochemist and parapsychologist. Some of his work has been quite controversial. Sheldrake conducted a number of surveys to find out how many pet owners had observed what they felt were psychic abilities in their pets. From the surveys, he found that 46 percent of dog owners had noticed this ability in their dogs in England; 45 percent had noticed the same ability in California. (Brown & Sheldrake, 1997; Sheldrake & Smart, 1997; Sheldrake et al, 1998).

A woman named Pamela Smart read about Sheldrake's research in 1994 and volunteered herself and her terrier Jaytee to be a part of it. According to Pamela, she and her family members had noticed that Jaytee seemed to anticipate Pamela's arrival home by up to half an hour, or more, even when she came home from work at unexpected times. Between May 1994 and February 1995, Pamela's family kept notes about the dog's behavior. They disregarded the times that Jaytee went to the window to bark at cats and for other similar reasons, and noted the times at which the dog seemed to be showing behavior that anticipated Pamela coming home. Pamela kept a record of her trips home, noting when she left to come home and her route, how she traveled, and what time she got home.

Sheldrake published this investigation in the *Journal of the Society for Psychical Research* in 1998, relying on the notes taken by the Smart family plus his own data from experiments with the dog. Based on the notes, Sheldrake found that Jaytee had a reaction ten minutes or more before Smart returned home 82 times. The dog showed no anticipatory reaction 14 times. There was a highly significant correlation between the time at which the dog reacted and the time at which Pamela started home from work. According to Sheldrake, the evidence showed that Jaytee's reactions depended on an influence from his owner that was detected by the dog in a manner currently unknown to science.

Of course, there are people who are still skeptical about the results of this experiment and who question the methods used, but this is the kind of experiment you can conduct with your own dogs to form your own opinions on the subject.

Tools

Dogs might not use tools, at least not without training from humans, but we use tools. We use them in our communication with dogs, too. Just as a rider uses a bridle and reins to communicate with a horse, the dog owner can use a collar and leash to communicate with a dog. We use whistles, crates, clickers, treats, rewards, and other training devices to communicate with our dogs because dogs are intelligent and they seem able to adapt to different kinds of learning. Here is a look at some of the tools we use for communicating with dogs:

Collars and leashes

Dog collars date back to predynastic times in ancient Egypt, if not earlier. Early collars were leather and were used on hunting dogs like salukis. Ancient Greeks and Romans also used collars on their dogs, and it has been common to use collars and leashes on dogs ever since.

There are many kinds of collars in use today: fashion collars, martingales (a collar-leash combo), slip collars or chain collars used for training, flat buckle collars, rolled leather collars, greyhound collars, and prong or pinch collars. There are even spiked collars for dogs, which have a history of being used on dogs in dogfights to protect the dog's throat.

Most people put a basic collar on a dog and never think about it again. But collars can contain information in case your dog gets lost such as your name, address, and phone number. You also can place your dog's rabies tag, license tags, and microchip tag on the collar to improve his chances of being returned to you.

People sometimes misunderstand training collars. For example, the slip collar or chain collar has been vilified in recent years since the advent of clicker training for dogs in the 1990s, but when used correctly, these collars do not hurt your dog. They should not be left on a dog at all times, but they can be used with success for training purposes. People who show their dogs often use a slip collar made of nylon or metal without harming the dogs.

Likewise, prong or pinch collars are often misunderstood. They might look fearsome because they have tines that touch a dog's neck, but they are not sharp, and they are not intended to hurt the dog. They put equal pressure all around the dog's throat and do not pull in a single place. If you have a large or eager dog, this kind of collar is often a good training tool. It can be used to teach a large dog not to pull on the leash, for example. They are also used by many sight hound (greyhound, saluki, whippet, and other similar breeds) owners to control their dogs when they take them lure coursing (chasing a mechanical lure for fun and sport in a field), when the dogs are eager and excited to run.

Choose a leash that is easy for you to manage and not one that is too long. Six feet is a good length, though you can use 4 feet to keep your dog closer to you. *Heeling and walking on a loose leash will be discussed in Chapter 5.*

Collars and leashes are important training tools for your dog. You can improve your communication with your dog by choosing the right collar and using it properly.

Grooming tools

Grooming can be a good time for you and your dog to bond and share each other's company. Or it can be a fairly unpleasant experience. It depends on how you groom your dog, how often you groom, how good you are at grooming, and the tools you use. Some dogs also like grooming more than other dogs. A dog might have one bad experience with grooming and can become difficult to groom forever afterward.

Some people prefer to take their dogs to a professional groomer, and that is always an option. If you plan to take your dog to a professional groomer, keep in mind that going to a grooming shop can be a stressful experience for some dogs. Make yourself aware of your dog's body language. Try to judge how your dog likes the groomer and the surroundings. Your dog might be nervous, but you should be able to tell if the groomer or other workers are making an effort to keep the dogs relaxed and comfortable. Look at the body language of the other dogs in the shop. Do they seem relaxed and at ease with the groomers working on them? Are the groomers paying attention to the dogs? You will be able to tell a lot just by watching your dog's reaction and looking at the other dogs.

It is not unusual for a dog to be nervous when he goes to the groomer, but a good groomer knows how to work with dogs in a calm, professional manner, so he or she can groom a dog with a minimum of stress.

Your other alternative is grooming your dog yourself. Many people groom their own dogs, especially if they have a dog with short hair or one that does not require any clipping. Your dog might still have mixed feelings about being groomed. Many dogs enjoy being brushed, but when it comes to having their nails trimmed or their ears cleaned, they become squeamish. If you plan to groom your own dog, pay careful attention to the body language your dog uses. He plainly will show you what he likes and does not like. This does not mean you can omit the tasks your dog does not like, such as having his nails trimmed. It just means that when you see your dog becoming nervous about having his paws touched, you know that you need to find a way to work with your dog so he feels better. Your dog's body language can alert you to potential problems so you can find solutions.

It is always easier to groom a dog if you keep up with the grooming and do it regularly. Most dogs will be kept well groomed if you brush them once or twice a week unless you have a breed that requires some specialized grooming such as an Afghan hound or a dog that needs to be brushed daily.

Brushing your dog can be soothing for both you and your dog, as long as you do not have to contend with mats and tangles. You can use a detangler following your dog's bath to reduce problems with tangles. If your dog does develop a mat, use a comb to gently unknot it.

Lots of communication goes on between a dog and an owner during a bath — not all of it fit for print, as some dogs heartily dislike getting a bath. You can usually help a dog enjoy getting a bath more if you start giving him baths often when he is a puppy and make it a fun time for him. Give him treats and play with him when he is in the tub.

If you have an adult dog that hates getting a bath, chances are that your dog's body language has been easy to read. You might have had to drag or carry him to the bathtub, for example. Perhaps he hides under the bed when it is bath time. Your dog might not ever love getting a bath, but you can make sure the bath is as nice as possible for him. Use the bathtub in your house and not a hose in the yard that puts out cold water. Make sure the water for the bath is warm and not too hot or cold. Your dog does not enjoy a blast of hot or cold water any more than you do. Many dogs do not like being in the tub because the floor is slippery and they slide so easily. Place a good rubber bath mat in the bottom of the tub and a large bath towel on top of the mat. This will give your dog as much security in the tub as possible. Be careful not to get the shampoo in your dog's eyes. Finally, a slow, gentle bath is better than blasting your dog with water that is too forceful because you are trying to get the bath over fast.

Speak soothingly to your dog during the bath and use slow, gentle strokes when you are bathing him. Remember that you are communicating with your body language, too; so let your dog know that the bath is supposed to be something good, and you are doing it because you care about him.

Many dogs are skittish about having their nails trimmed, usually because they have had a bad experience. Start picking up and touching your puppy's paws when he is young. Make it normal for you to handle his paws and toes. Use a pair of clippers to trim the nails when your dog is relaxed. Be sure to give him treats for each nail you trim. In some cases, a dog might behave better if you use a nail grinder to sand his nails down. There are several popular models sold now to pet owners, such as PediPaws, which can be found at popular pet stores. These sanders are similar to the professional models pet groomers and dog show people use.

Watch for signs that your dog is stressed when you are doing his nails. Signals might include your dog turning his head away from you, nervously licking his nose, glancing away from you, yawning, or trying to remove his paw from your hand. If your dog is stressed, you can acknowledge his signals. This is not the time to get mad at your dog or try to forcefully trim his nails. Pet him. Talk to him. Pick up his paw and hold it for a few seconds. If your dog has had a bad experience with nail trimming, it is a good idea to only remove the tiniest tips of the nails so there will not be any possibility that you can hurt your dog. If you do this often, your dog will become accustomed to you handling his paws and trimming his nails. You gradually will begin to shorten the nails. There is no rule that says you have to trim all of your dog's nails at one time. You can trim one paw per day if that is what you and your dog negotiate.

Remember to brush your dog's teeth regularly. Your dog should enjoy this grooming task. Use a doggy toothbrush and doggy toothpaste. Do not use human toothpaste. It contains xylitol, an artificial sweetener that is harmful to dogs. Doggy toothpaste is made in flavors dogs love such as peanut butter, chicken, beef, and liver. Most dogs consider doggy toothpaste a treat.

Finally, check your dog's ears regularly and clean as needed. They should be pale pink, and there should not be any odor to them. Some dogs are not fond of having their ears cleaned, but it should not be painful for them. If your dog does not like having his ears cleaned, watch his body language again, and it should tell you how he feels about it.

Your dog might display a variety of body language while you are doing some of these things, but they are necessary to take care of your dog.

Crates

A crate is another tool we use to communicate with our dogs. Crates are commonly used for housetraining, to provide a sleeping place for a dog, to give a dog a place to "hang out" when  the house is hectic, and to protect the dog when traveling in a vehicle or when flying on an airplane. If you ever intend to take your medium or large dog with you on a plane, he will need to fly in a crate. Only the smallest dogs can fly in the cabin in a carry-on bag.

For training purposes, you can use a crate to give your dog a time-out if he needs a break. If your dog is a chewer or prone to destroying things in the house, you can have him spend some time in the crate, where he can chew on more appropriate items if you need to leave the house for a couple of hours. If your puppy is playing too roughly and nipping people, you can give him a half-hour time-out in the crate until he calms down. These are good ways to reinforce some of the things your dog needs to learn. Your dog's crate can be an important aid in your communication with your dog.

Author Experiences: Pearl

Sometimes dogs are not subtle at all. Pearl is not a subtle dog. Pearl is concerned about her breakfast every morning, and for a while, she used to wake me up at 4:30 a.m. by standing on my chest and bouncing. When a 50-pound dog bounces on you at that time of the morning, it is not pleasant. But she was getting her message across. I finally got MY message across ("I do not like this behavior!") by putting Pearl in her crate when she bounced on me at any time. Now Pearl waits until later (5 a.m.), and she has learned to be a little subtler with her communication. She sits beside my bed and stares at me until I wake up. Sometimes she pokes me with her nose or paw. And sometimes all of my dogs join her, and I wake up with five dogs staring at me. You would be surprised at how hard it is to sleep with five dogs staring at your face, sniffing, and snorting.

But that is how we negotiate things in our house. At least Pearl is not bouncing on my chest any longer, and I get to sleep half an hour later. We are communicating.

You do not need to worry that your dog will associate the crate with punishment or negative things if he uses the crate often for other things such as taking naps or traveling with you. Many owners leave the crate door open most of the time so their dog can go in and out of the crate as he wishes. Lots of dogs enjoy napping in a crate. You can make it comfortable for your dog by placing a faux sheepskin mat or some blankets in the bottom of the crate. Put some of your dog's toys in the crate along with some safe things to chew on, such as Nylabones® or a Kong® toy stuffed with peanut butter or cream cheese. This setup can keep a dog happy for hours.

Toys and games

Dogs are one of the few species that continues to have a strong play drive into their adult lives. They share this trait with humans. You can use your dog's playfulness as a way to bond with him and strengthen the communication between you.

Dogs love all kinds of toys: the ever-popular ball, rope toys, stuffed animals, chew toys, squeaky toys, Frisbees — you name it. Dogs love to play with just about anything that can possibly be a toy. Spending time playing with your dog is a good way to keep your dog active, get some exercise for yourself, and get closer to your dog.

You might notice that when dogs play, they tend to relax their body language and social rules a bit. Two unfamiliar dogs that meet normally will be rather formal with each other; they will go through a ritual of sniffing each other and assessing who has a higher status. However, when dogs play, some of the rules are relaxed. If there is a little bumping or if one is accidentally nipped, the dogs usually take it in stride unless one gets huffy. At that point, the dogs tend to separate for a few minutes, and they might or might not continue their games.

When your dog plays with you, he also will adopt a looser attitude. He will not be reading your body language and social cues as closely as usual. Instead, he will be running, playing, and chasing the ball, like anyone playing a game. Do not be offended if your dog accidentally slams into you or scratches you. It is not intentional. However, this is one reason why children always should be supervised when they play with dogs. Your dog does not understand that a child can be hurt by this kind of play, so it is important for an adult to make sure no one gets hurt.

You also can play with your dog using interactive games. These games are intended for the owner to play with the dog. Many of these games challenge the dog's thinking abilities. Games of this kind include the Buster® Cube, which involves you putting treats into a cube that your dog then rolls around to get the treats to come out. Dog toy designer Nina Ottosson (**www.nina-ottosson.com**) also makes interactive games for dogs. The games often feature blocks or bricks that the dog has to move with his nose or paw so he can find hidden treats. Sometimes the games have levels that increase with difficulty as your dog becomes good at each task. You will need to play these games with your dog to make sure your dog does not eat the blocks to get to the treats. Games that provide mental stimulation for your dog offer good opportunities for you to enhance your communication with him. These games require close interaction between you and your dog. You need to observe your dog's behavior to help him play the games. They are fun for you and your dog, and they can improve your communication skills.

Training devices

Another way we communicate with dogs is through training devices. These devices can include clickers for clicker training, whistles used by trainers to train dogs for herding and other work, bark collars, collars to train hunting dogs, wireless fences, and even agility equipment and other specialized equipment for different dog sports and activities. Someone showing dogs might use "Happy Legs"  (**www.happylegs.com**) to teach their dog to stand still and keep all four legs in place. Happy Legs is a training aid that lets you place your dog's paws on small blocks so he learns how to stand correctly for the show ring. The owner offers praise and treats to the dog as he learns how to stand and hold his position. This would be a specialized training device for someone who shows dogs. The owner and dog would be communicating about where the dog should place his paws and how he should stand. (This is not as easy as it sounds.)

A hunter might need some special equipment for training his dog to hunt such as a check cord. The check cord is a long rope, nylon or cotton, that attaches to the dog's collar when he is being trained to be steady when he finds birds. Many young dogs are excited about finding a bird and might not wait for the hunter to catch up with them. Instead, they might flush the bird, making it fly. Obviously, it is not good in a hunting situation for the bird to be flushed before the hunter is ready, so the dog needs to hold his point until the hunter comes. When the dog is on the check cord, the hunter can stay closer and communicate with him by talking to him and urging him to be still and wait.

These are just a few examples of the way owners can use training devices to communicate with their dogs during these specialized activities. Of course, the use of the clicker is widespread, and it is easy to see how it can be used as a communication device. It is used to "mark" the behavior of the dog that the owner wants to encourage, and then a food reward is given. Dogs understand this kind of communication — and most things related to food — quite well.

Motivational treats and rewards

One of the best ways we have of communicating with dogs is through motivational treats and rewards. As far as your dog is concerned, these are always positive, so if you give your dog a treat, he will remember it and will associate it with good things. You are the giver of treats, dinner, and probably most of his food, which makes you a good thing. Dogs are not entirely food-motivated, and some dogs  might prefer some other kind of reward, but most dogs are happy to respond to food as a reward. They understand that when you give them food, you like them, and you are happy with them. That kind of communication is easy.

But perhaps your dog would prefer some other kind of reward. Some dogs like to have their belly rubbed, or they would like to play with their favorite toy. If you have a retriever, then he might prefer a game of fetch instead of a food reward. Some dogs would rather do the things they were bred to do than eat. Your dog might like to go for a run instead of having a food reward. The point is that you know your dog best, and you will know what motivates him and what he likes best as a reward.

If your dog is motivated by treats and food rewards, then find out what kind of treats he likes best, especially if you intend to do some training with him. Your dog might work for hot dog bits as treats but perhaps he will give his best effort if you use some baked liver. Or, maybe he goes crazy for cheese? Save some of his special favorites for when you are asking him to do something that takes plenty of focus and concentration, and then give him a big payoff.

We have many different methods for communicating with our dogs. From talking to our dogs and using body language, they can easily read, to touching them, grooming them, and using tools and training devices, humans have developed countless ways to communicate with dogs.

CHAPTER THREE

Socialization

Socialization is the process of introducing your puppy or dog to all of the strange and wonderful things in the world that could make him anxious or nervous and letting him see that he does not have to be afraid. The more things you can show your puppy or dog in a controlled way, the better.

The Importance of Socialization

Puppy socialization is one of the most important parts of training your dog. The things your puppy learns when he is young stay with him all his life. With puppy socialization, your puppy learns that people are friendly, and he gains confidence in exploring the world. Puppy socialization is the key to having a happy, well-adjusted dog for a pet.

Early puppy development

Puppies are born with their eyes and ears sealed shut. Their eyes begin to open when they are about 2 weeks old, and they begin to hear soon after that. During the first few days of life, they are helpless. They have a sense of smell, and they can sense warmth and cold. This helps them find their mother so they can stay warm and nurse. Otherwise, puppies are dependent on their mother caring for them. Their mother nurses them and washes them to clean up after them. At this stage, puppies can only wiggle and crawl around their whelping area (the place where they were born).

Once a puppy's eyes open and he can hear, he starts to become physically stronger and starts to explore his area. However, he is still completely dependent on his mother. Everything  he learns, he learns from her. In a few days, he begins to be more aware of his littermates and learns from his interactions with them, too.

The puppy has a good deal to learn in the few weeks he spends with his mother and littermates. Most of this time is spent teaching the puppy how to become a dog. Puppies learn to bark, to play with their brothers and sisters without hurting each other (this is called bite inhibition), and other lessons their mother considers important. Some mother dogs are strict with their puppies, and others are gentle and permissive, but this period is mostly the same for all puppies because it is based on canine instincts.

When your puppy comes to live with you between the age of 8 and 12 weeks, this is all he has learned. He knows some of the basics of being a dog, though he is not an expert at dog communication. If he meets a strange dog, he will probably not know how to greet him properly. He does not know how to interact with friendly dogs that are not his littermates. He might have spent time with his breeder being petted, but he is probably not housetrained nor does he know much about the things in the house or yard that could frighten him. He probably has not been to many places outside his home. It is up to you to teach him what he needs to learn and to provide him with good learning opportunities.

Puppies who learn at an early age how to interact with other dogs and how to meet friendly strangers, and puppies that go places and see things are considered well socialized. These dogs develop healthy self-confidence and are less likely to experience behavior problems as adult dogs.

Puppy developmental stages

From the time your puppy is born, he is constantly developing physically, mentally, and emotionally. Nature has preordained much of your puppy's development — the age at which he will stop nursing and start eating solid food; the age when he will start exploring his surroundings; and the age when he will start getting adult teeth. His behavior will be related to some of his physical changes.

Puppies go through many stages in their first couple of years, based on findings from researchers Scott and Fuller's studies in the 1960s (*Genetics and the Social Behavior of the Dog*) and confirmed by other research since then. They go through several of these stages before you ever bring your puppy home with you. All of the stages are important and help form your puppy's personality.

Stage 1

Stage 1 of your puppy's development occurs when your puppy is 2 to 3 weeks old and still with his mother. Your puppy's mother is the single biggest early influence on him. This is one

reason why the temperament of the mother is so important

to your puppy's development. During Stage 1, your puppy will transition from being born blind and deaf to having his eyes and ears open so he can start learning about the world. He will begin to crawl around the whelping box and venture away from his mother more. And he can start to recognize his mother, brothers, and sisters. If you put soft toys in the litter box, the puppy will start to notice them slightly, though it is too early for him to play. Many breeders start doing early neural stimulation with puppies during this time to stimulate their senses. They can stroke their puppies' toes or hold them upside down for a few seconds. This has been shown to give puppies a head start and help them learn better as they get older.

Stage 2

Stage 2 takes place between 3 and 4 weeks old. During this time, your puppy's senses are developing rapidly. He starts to notice everything around him. He starts to recognize you, his mother, littermates, and other people who visit. Your puppy is learning how to be a little dog during this period. He will start barking, trying to run, and playing with his brothers and sisters. Make sure this is a safe time for your puppy because bad events that happen during this stage can leave a lasting impression.

Stage 3

Stage 3 is a critical time for your puppy. This period occurs between 4 and 7 weeks old. At this time, he is learning social skills and how to interact with his mother, littermates, and even with you. He learns about playing and bite inhibition. During this stage, the mother also will wean the puppies so your puppy will start to learn about discipline. When your puppy tries to nurse, usually between 5 and 7 weeks old, his mother might snap at him or even bite him. She also will start teaching the puppies other things they need to know, such as pack structure and to accept leadership. You can start weaning the puppies or offering them mushy food at about 3 to 4 weeks old. You should handle the puppies often, but they should not be taken away from their mother and littermates before they are 7 weeks old at the earliest. Eight weeks is better for larger dogs. Smaller dogs need to stay with their mothers and littermates until they are 10 to 12 weeks of age. This is an important time in their life when their mother is teaching them how to behave. If you take a puppy away too early, he is apt to be nervous and anxious for the rest of his life and might have trouble with socialization and learning later. They are also more likely to bark and have other behavior problems later.

Puppies can learn social skills most easily between 3 and 16 weeks old. They need to learn skills from their mother, their breeder, and you when you bring your puppy home. Do not let this important learning stage be wasted. It is best to leave puppies with their mother and littermates for as much of this time as possible.

Stage 4

Stage 4 begins when a puppy is about 8 weeks old and continues until he is about 3 months old. During this stage, puppies are afraid of lots of things. They learn quickly during this time, but between about 8 and 10 weeks, they tend to be fearful. They can even become afraid  of things they were not afraid of previously. During this time, do not use punishment on your puppy, or your puppy will be afraid of you for a long time. Do not yell at your puppy, and try to avoid any scary events.

You can start to teach your puppy some basic commands during this time, such as the basic obedience commands. And your puppy is ready to start housetraining. You also can start leash training. Make sure you do not leave your puppy alone during this time because this is a social time for him, and he needs to be around people.

Stage 5

Stage 5 takes place when your puppy 3 to 4 months old. Your puppy will go through a toddler stage at this time. He might ignore the things he has just learned. Housetraining can be a challenge. He is just learning all the fun things he can do. He might play bite, so you will need to help him relearn bite inhibition. He might play too roughly, so this is a good time to crate train. Time-outs work, too, just as they do for little  kids. Play with your puppy, but do not get into a power struggle at this age. He will only learn bad lessons.

Stage 6

Stage 6 happens between the age of 4 and 6 months. Your puppy will seem willful and independent at this time. He also will be teething, so you need to make sure he has plenty of acceptable things to chew on. Otherwise, he is going to destroy your things. At this age, your puppy might try to show some dominant behavior, which is not acceptable. This is especially true if you have children or other pets. In other words, your puppy is going to be a brat at this time and try to test boundaries. Expect it. If you have not already started some obedience training with your puppy, this is a good time to start. Enroll in a puppy training class. Do not allow your puppy off leash in an open area. He is not going to come when you call him at this age.

Stage 7

Stage 7 is the final stage of your puppy's development. It lasts from the time your puppy is about 6 months old until he is about 18 months old. Most of the serious naughty behavior will pass by this time, but your puppy is young and feels frisky. He will get into trouble. He will play with things he should not. He still will tear things up, but he will not be challenging you all the time anymore. He is no longer acting like a little rebel. He is, however, still learning important things about being an adult dog.

During these months, your dog is starting to look, and sometimes act, like an adult dog, but he is not fully grown yet, so keep your expectations reasonable until your dog is about 18 months old. Your dog will not be fully mature until about that time. Continue training your dog and teaching him how you would like him to behave in terms of manners.

How to Socialize Your Puppy

As you can see, your puppy goes through several stages when he is open to socialization and some stages where he will be particularly prone to being fearful. These are approximations based on studies with many dogs. During these times, and throughout his youth, it is important that you socialize your puppy well so he will not become permanently fearful. Dogs who develop fears when they are young are more likely to be anxious as adults. This can lead to problems such as separation anxiety, destructive chewing, and other behavioral problems later on, especially when the dog is left alone. Dogs that are well socialized when they are young are much more likely to be confident as adults and will be well-adjusted and well-behaved adult dogs.

Once your puppy goes home with you, it will be up to you to help him develop his confidence by introducing him to things that could frighten him so he can see he has nothing to fear. Show him things such as vacuum cleaners; make sure he knows about TVs, radios, and stereos; teach him about lawn mowers (and to stay away from them); and teach him about car rides and the family cat. Anything that makes a loud noise could be something that would frighten your pup, so it should be on your list of things to teach your puppy about. Also, introduce him to things that appear and disappear suddenly, such as umbrellas. Teach him about everything in your home.

When you introduce your puppy to new things, be positive and cheerful. This will give your puppy confidence and show him how he should react to things. Do not coddle him or act like he has anything to fear. If your puppy is scared of something, give him a pat and laugh it off. The goal is to give your puppy confidence so he can grow up to be a confident adult, not to help him hide from things. Set a good example for your puppy, and show him how to react.

Taking your puppy places

Once your puppy becomes comfortable with the things in your home, you can move on to the outside world. However, before you start taking your puppy to places outside your home, make sure he has had his second set of vaccinations from the vet. You might be meeting dogs and other puppies that have not been vaccinated, so keep your own puppy safe. Remember, too, that  not every dog you meet will be friendly. Learn to keep your puppy back from other dogs until you assess whether the other dog would welcome meeting your puppy. This can save your puppy from being snapped at or bitten. Keep your puppy on a leash, and ask permission from the other dog's owner before going up to another dog.

You can begin socializing your puppy in the outside world by visiting places such as pet supply stores that welcome dogs. You can let your puppy (on a leash) go up and down the aisles to see the toys and supplies. Be sure to take some treats with you so you can encourage friendly strangers to pet your puppy. That way when your puppy allows them to pet him, they can offer your puppy a treat, too. Cap off your visit by letting your puppy pick out a favorite toy.

You also can visit parks with your puppy. Dog parks are not recommended. The play at dog parks can be too rough for puppies, and not all owners keep a close eye on their dogs. But a park with leashed dogs is a good setting for your puppy to meet friendly people. Your puppy can see more people who can pet him and give him treats. Your puppy also can see new things including wildlife.

Going to puppy preschool classes

Many people like to enroll a puppy in puppy preschool or puppy kindergarten classes. These are basic classes for socialization that also teach some obedience. They are only for puppies, so your puppy will have some playmates, too. He also will get petting from the other owners — which means more

socialization. These classes are a good way for your puppy to make dog and people friends and become more outgoing. Kennel clubs, pet stores, and dog training centers often offer them.

Do not stop socializing your puppy just because he has been out and about some at an early age. Continue to socialize your puppy until he is an adult dog. Dogs can become fearful again when they are several months old if you do not continue to socialize them, so keep taking your dog with you when you go places and encourage people to pet him. All your socialization will pay off when you have a happy, confident adult dog later on.

How to Socialize an Adult Dog

So far, we have been discussing how to socialize a puppy. However, many people today are taking on the responsibility of adopting older dogs. Some of these dogs come from rescues or animal shelters, or they might be re-homed from breeders or other sources. In these circumstances, dogs might not have been well socialized when they were puppies or they might need to be resocialized to help them overcome negative experiences in their lives. Fortunately, most dogs are resilient enough to be socialized later in life.

If you are trying to socialize an adult dog, you can follow the same advice offered for socializing puppies. The developmental stages will not apply to your dog, but, otherwise, you can help your adult dog rebuild his confidence. You will need to proceed slowly because instead of working with a puppy that has no fears already learned, you will be working with a dog that already has some fears and possible behavior problems.

Begin by checking your adult dog out at home and noticing if he has any fears. How does he react around common household objects? Do noises bother him? See how he reacts to TVs, radios, stereos, vacuum cleaners, and other things that can be loud. Is he afraid of umbrellas that pop open, men with hats, or other unexpected things? You will probably find out some of these quirks in the course of living with your dog, but you can test him to see how he reacts to other happenings.

If you find that your adult dog is afraid of some ordinary things at home, you can work with him to desensitize him to the objects or noises. For instance, if your dog is afraid of the vacuum cleaner, try taking it outside and showing it to your dog. It might seem less frightening to your dog outdoors where there is more space. Place some dog treats on it. Encourage your dog to check it out when it is quiet. Work up to touching your dog with it and rewarding him. Your dog might never like the vacuum, but you should reach the point where you can use it in the house without your dog being terrified.

If your adult dog is afraid of people, it will also take some time to help him overcome his fear. Do not pressure him or force him to allow people to pet him. Take him to the same kind of places you would take a puppy for socialization, such as hanging out in the parking lot at the pet store. Give friendly people some treats so they can offer them to your dog. But leave it up to your dog whether or not he wants to let them pet him. This can take some time if your dog has had bad experiences in his past, but if you are patient, your dog should begin to allow friendly people to give him a treat and pat him.

With dogs that have had bad experiences, it is recommended that people do not pat them on the head, which can be perceived as threatening. Instead, pet them from the side or under the throat.

One of the best ways to socialize adult dogs and help rebuild their confidence is by enrolling them in a training class. Training helps to build confidence; it strengthens the communication and bond between you and your dog; and it is a good way to socialize your dog. Try these suggestions for socializing an adult dog, and you should see improvement in his confidence.

Socialization is the foundation for teaching your dog manners, for learning to communicate with your dog, and for training your dog. It continues the lessons that your puppy begins learning from his mother and littermates. It is up to you to socialize your puppy and introduce him to the world so he will be in the right frame of mind to learn what you have to teach him.

Once you have begun socializing your puppy, you can start working on basic training. The next chapter will look at the various training methods that are used today and what kind of options you have for training your dog. Some methods are likely to be better than others for you and your dog and will do more to improve your communication.

CHAPTER FOUR

Effective Ways of Communicating With Your Dog Through Training

Humans probably have been training dogs almost as long as dogs have been domesticated. The Egyptians, Greeks, and Romans kept hounds for hunting. The Romans used mastiff-type dogs for war. And dogs have been used for flock guarding and herding for millennia. All of these dogs would have required training for their work.

Through the centuries, dogs were used in many ways to help humans, but it was not until the beginning of the 20th century that dog training began to be studied seriously and applied to dogs. The development of the human field of psychology, and later, the study of animal behavior and ethology, also have had an impact on dog training. Today there are several different kinds of dog training methods in addition to specialized training for dogs such as guide dogs, hunting dogs, search and rescue dogs, and other dogs engaged in advanced activities. Training your dog is an excellent way to strengthen the bond that exists between you, but differences exist between the training methods. Some methods will work for some dogs better than others. All the methods have their pros and cons.

Different Types of Dog Training

Three main dog training methods are used today, in theory. In practice, many trainers and owners take elements of the three theories and use what works for their dogs. The three main theories used for dog training today are traditional dog training, sometimes called the Koehler Method after the man who literally wrote the book on it; dog whispering, which trainer Cesar Millan made popular; and positive  reinforcement. Positive reinforcement is most often used in the form of clicker training, but it can be used with any system that works with praise and rewards.

Traditional dog training

Modern dog training began with Colonel Conrad Most, who started training police dogs in Germany in 1906. In 1910, he wrote the revolutionary book *Training Dogs*, one of the very first dog training books. Most allowed dogs to make a mistake and then punished them for it, which was a new idea at the time. Most's ideas were put into practice with the military dogs trained for the German army during World War I, where they produced well-trained dogs that were admired by American soldiers. Following the war, Most's methods started to become known in the United States.

William Koehler trained dogs for the U.S. Military until the end of World War II. Following the war, he taught classes and individual dog training classes. In 1962, he wrote the book *The Koehler Method of Dog Training*. Koehler's method uses many of the same approaches as Most used. It is based on correction and punishment of the dog. This method is still popular today, and trainers continue to be trained in the Koehler method. If you took a dog training class between the 1940s and the 1990s, you probably used this method with your dog.

The Koehler Method, or traditional dog training, as it is often called, uses a slip collar on the dog or a chain link collar. Nothing is inherently painful or cruel about these collars, but they must be used correctly. Some people make the mistake of putting the collars on backward. The collar should be put on the dog so the loop faces to the right. It should form a "p"

and not a "q." Some people can accidentally hurt their dog if they pull on the leash and collar continually. The collar is only supposed to be pulled on with a quick, jerking motion and then immediately released. Chain link collars should not be left on a dog all the time because a dog could catch the collar on something and choke himself. They are only meant for training.

Traditional dog training relies on negative reinforcement and punishment. Negative reinforcement serves to strengthen a good behavior because when the dog behaves in an appropriate way, an unpleasant situation is stopped or avoided. If you push on your dog's hindquarters to get him to sit down, the pressure will be removed when your dog finally sits. He will be more likely to sit in the future in order to avoid the pressure.

Punishment is defined as an unpleasant consequence of a particular behavior.

Traditional dog training is usually geared toward teaching obedience lessons. It is not as effective when it comes to working on behavior problems.

The Koehler method does allow the dog to make a mistake and then punish the dog. For example, if you tell your dog to "heel," you would start walking; your dog should walk quietly by your side and then sit by your knee when you stop walking. If your dog continues to move when you stop, you would give a quick, corrective jerk with the leash. This should remind your dog that he is supposed to sit when you stop walking, and he should sit. The next time you stop walking during the heel maneuver, your dog will be more likely to remember to sit.

As with all dog training methods, the Koehler method has its pros and cons. Those who favor positive reinforcement often dislike the fact that this method uses punishment and correction. Some people think that this method is harsh. In fact, it can be a demanding method for some dogs and some breeds. If you have a soft-natured dog, then he might not do well with this training method. However, for some breeds that are more likely to be strong-willed and domineering, this method can be effective. Trainers who use this method emphasize that dogs trained using the Koehler method are more likely to remember what they learn. The use of the chain collar, sometimes called a "choke" collar, is problematic for some critics. If an owner pulls on the collar continually, it becomes ineffective as a training tool, and it can injure the dog's throat.

It is possible to achieve remarkable training success using the Koehler method. Koehler was an animal trainer for Disney Studios for more than 20 years and was responsible for many of the great animal performances in their films. Many thousands of dogs have been well trained, and happily trained, using this method.

Today, many people believe traditional dog training is too austere. Many trainers and owners prefer methods that rely more on praise and reward as you find in positive reinforcement.

They find that dogs learn better when they are happier and more excited about their lessons. Trainers still teach the Koehler method or traditional dog training. If you prefer this kind of training, you can find trainers who teach this method.

Dog whispering

Dog whispering is not a training method as much as it is a method of behavior analysis and communication. Dog whispering is based on ethology, the study of the behaviors of species under natural situations such as wolves living in packs in the wild. Dog whisperers claim to communicate with dogs by understanding their  body language and communicating with them. They claim that dog behavior is based on wolf pack behavior and that there is a pack hierarchy at work between dogs and humans in a home. Dog whisperers say that humans must establish themselves as dominant, in the "alpha" role in the pack, or as the pack leader.

Techniques used for the human to establish the dominant role include shaking a puppy by the scruff of the neck, as a mother wolf does to a cub, and rolling a subordinate pack member (the dog) over onto his back to expose his stomach. These are methods for the human to display dominance over the dog.

This theory gained popularity in the 1980s. The most well-known practitioner of dog whispering is Cesar Millan. The National Geographic Channel airs his program, *The Dog Whisperer*. He also has written a number of books and has celebrity clients. However, he has been taken to task by the International Association of Animal Behavior Consultants for some of the scenes on his program, particularly scenes involving children and animals that could have endangered the children and which the IAABC deemed inadvisable for the dogs as well. Many other dog trainers have also criticized his methods for harshness and violence toward dogs. Jan Fennell is another well-known dog trainer who uses dog whispering techniques.

Does dog whispering work? According to some experts, if it works, it works because the dogs are scared. Most dog trainers and experts do not consider dog whispering to be an actual training technique. You cannot teach your dog obedience commands using dog whispering. People who use dog whispering say they are engaging in communication with their dogs and that they can work on behavior problems by reading their dogs' body language. These trainers say it is also important to work with the people who own the dogs so they can learn how to "be the alpha" and make their dogs obey.

Trainers who practice dog whispering also encourage owners to make sure their dogs get plenty of exercise. This keeps them from getting into trouble in the home. This is good advice for all owners. People who engage in dog whispering also emphasize that dogs are not small humans and should not be treated as substitutes for children. Again, this is good advice for all dog owners. Dogs should be treated like dogs. Anything else will confuse them and eventually lead to behavior problems. Practitioners of dog whispering say that humans must assert themselves to be leaders of the "pack." If owners do not do this, they say, then dogs will take over as the alpha or leader in the home, which will lead to problems.

Critics of dog whispering believe that trainers who work with dogs in this way are more experienced with dogs than the owners and can get dogs to behave for them using these methods. Dogs might comply with the trainers out of fear. However, when the owners try the same methods with the dogs, they might not be able to achieve success. Some of the methods used might be dangerous when used by people without much dog experience.

Other criticism of dog whispering comes from the fact that it claims to be based on wolf behavior. One critic, noted veterinarian and dog trainer Dr. Ian Dunbar, says this is like learning to parent a human child by watching chimpanzees.

Dog whispering as practiced by Millan has many fans, but this approach has some problems. For one thing, no research backs up these theories. Some of the information applied in dog whispering seems to be based only on popular myth and not on scientific studies. Wolves, and even dogs in the wild, do not live in the kind of social hierarchy assumed by these trainers. L. David Mech is a senior scientist with the Biological Resources Division, U.S. Geological Survey, and an adjunct professor in the Department of Fisheries, Wildlife and Conservation Biology, and Ecology, Evolution and Behavior at the University of Minnesota. He has been studying wolves since 1958. In his paper "Alpha Status, Dominance, and Division of Labor in Wolf Packs," he explains that wolves have familial relationships, and they are not based on dominance as described in dog whispering.

Other researchers agree with Mech. Instead of living in a pack with alphas and betas, as described in dog whispering, the most recent research shows that wolves and dogs live in family units with parental figures (a father and mother) that act as the leaders of the pack. Younger animals are subordinate because they are younger family members, not because they are necessarily weaker or of less social standing. The family situation is similar to a human family. For a human being to insert himself into such a family dynamic as the "alpha" makes no sense.

That is not to say that humans should not be in charge in their homes. Humans should, of course, set reasonable rules in a household and expect dogs to follow them. But for trainers to advise clients to assume a wolf or dog-like role is suspect advice, especially when it is based on misinformation.

The use of physical force on dogs has also been shown to backfire. The latest findings from the American Veterinary Society of Animal Behavior show that when you use aggression, dominance, or any kind of physical force against a dog, you are far more likely to cause a dog to react with aggression toward humans, even if the dog has never displayed aggression before. Advising people to use physical force with dogs is not a good idea. There are better ways of dealing with dogs that are having behavior problems.

Research has shown that fear and anxiety are at the root of many behavior problems in dogs. Working on these problems, instead of trying to assert yourself as the "alpha," will help your dog overcome his problems.

Dog whispering can be tough, and it is based on ideas about dominance. Dog whisperers always have maintained that their approach is based on natural wolf behavior but scientific research does not back them up. There are some common sense ideas found in dog whispering about setting boundaries with your dog, not letting your dog take advantage of you, and being the boss in your home, but it is not necessary to accept some of the more questionable tenets of dog whispering in order to use these ideas.

Positive reinforcement

Positive reinforcement training can be applied to many kinds of animals and even to humans. It has been used to teach children in schools and to teach chickens and dolphins. The basic premise is that you praise and reward the individual for doing what you want them to do, and you ignore the things that you do not want them to do (or the incorrect responses).

For example, if you were teaching your dog to shake your hand, you would praise and reward him every time he gives you his paw when you ask for it. When you ask for his paw and he does not do anything or he licks your hand, you ignore him and try again. You do not punish or correct, but the praise and reward have to be big when he does things correctly. This kind of training emphasizes keeping the dog happy.

Training is like playing. It should be fun for the dog and for the owner/trainer.

Positive reinforcement is a form of operant conditioning, which psychologist B.F. Skinner developed. Operant conditioning uses behavioral principles to condition certain responses in animals (or people). Psychologists Keller and Marian Breland then further developed positive reinforcement in the 1940s for use in animals. They tried to develop their ideas to use them for commercial dog training, but no one was interested at that time. So, they turned to training for the Navy and trained dolphins. They also trained animals for TV and commercials.

The Brelands continued training for many years, but it was not until the 1980s when Karen Pryor, another marine animal trainer, wrote a book called *Don't Shoot The Dog*, that many people became aware of positive reinforcement techniques.

This book was not actually about dog training, despite the title, but the principles of positive reinforcement were soon being applied to training dogs.

One of the additions to positive reinforcement training is the clicker. The clicker is a small, handheld device that allows the owner/trainer to click at the exact moment a dog does what the owner/trainer wants him to do. This helps the dog to identify what he is doing right so he can do it again. The clicker is just a $2 to $3 item, but it is extremely helpful in training your dog.

Advocates of positive reinforcement say that dogs learn quickly with these methods because they are fun for dogs. There is no punishment, no fear, and no pain. Most dogs enjoy learning with positive reinforcement.

Critics claim that positive reinforcement emphasizes food rewards and that dogs will not learn without food. They say that when there is no food, the dogs will not learn and will not reliably repeat what they have learned.

In defense of positive reinforcement, the reward offered does not have to be food. You can use any kind of reward that your dog likes: You can play with your dog, pet him, give him hugs, or whatever makes him happy. But most people do use food treats as rewards. There is nothing wrong with giving your dog food treats as rewards.

The positive reinforcement approach is good for both obedience training and for behavior modification. You can effectively teach your dog basic obedience and change his behavior with positive reinforcement. It is easy to teach your dog to sit, stay, heel, and other obedience commands using positive reinforcement (especially using a clicker). And positive reinforcement works well for teaching your dog not to chew on things or jump on people or with some of the other behavior problems that are typical for dogs. *Chapter 7 will discuss in further detail how to correct negative behaviors.*

Positive reinforcement is also easy for many people to use no matter what their age or size. Children can use a clicker to train a dog. Disabled people have trained dogs using positive reinforcement. You do not require any particular strength or physical abilities to train a dog using positive reinforcement.

Clicker training

Clicker training is not difficult. Your dog does something you like, whatever that might be, and you click to "mark" it. The click lets the dog know exactly what it is that you like, then you reward him. If you do this several times, your dog will make the connection and know why he is getting a reward.

If you time things correctly and are consistent, clicker training is usually easy and a lot of fun for you and your dog. Most dogs learn well with clicker training. It seems more like a game to them than other kinds of training, and a reward is involved. There is no yelling or punishment. There is no correction. If your dog does not do what you want, then you ignore what he is doing until he does do what you want, and you can "click" to mark the behavior and reward it.

The theory behind what you are doing is that you are conditioning your dog to do something and to be motivated to repeat the performance. Your dog learns that he can earn rewards by doing things that you want him to do.

Clicker training seems to work with almost all dogs, from young puppies to old dogs, including dogs that have behavior problems. You are changing your dog's behavior in small steps. Even complicated tricks can be taught by teaching your dog one small step at a time using a clicker, so you are teaching your dog in segments he can understand. And clicker training is something virtually all people can learn to do regardless of their age or health condition. Even small children can learn to clicker train a dog.

The most important thing with clicker training is to practice getting your timing right. If you click too early or too late, you can confuse your dog and he will not know what he did to please you or to get his reward. Timing and consistency are important in any kind of training, including clicker training.

You also have to remember to reinforce your dog's behavior with the reward. Do not be stingy with rewards, especially in the learning stages.

Clicker Training At Work

Getting started with clicker training is simple. You need a clicker. They are inexpensive and are sold in many pet stores and at dog show vendor booths, or you can buy one online from a dog supply website. Many pet stores, kennel clubs, and animal shelters offer training classes. You can check  with them to see if they teach clicker training and if they have clickers for sale.

You also will need something your dog likes for treats. It is best to use small treats so your dog will not fill up on them quickly. You can use hot dog bits, pieces of cheese, pieces of dog food, or training treats from the pet store.

You use the clicker two ways. You can get your dog to do something you like and click. Or you can wait until your dog does something you like on his own and then click. For example, you can lure your dog into a sitting position with a piece of food and click. Or, you can wait until your dog sits on his own and click. Either way will work to teach your dog to sit using the clicker. When your dog does something you like and you click, that is called "marking" the behavior.

Do not forget the reinforcement. When your dog does what you like and you click, give him the positive reinforcement — often in the form of a treat. Suppose you wait until your dog sits on his own, you click and then give your dog a treat. Now, just add the command "sit," and you have taught your dog to sit using the clicker. Reinforcement is about adding and taking away things your dog likes as motivation. It is often about treats, but it is also about praise, going for walks, giving toys, and other things your dog loves.

Gradually, as your dog learns his new behavior, the clicker is no longer needed.

Remember that as with any other kind of training, clicker training requires practice. It is easy and fun for a dog to learn this way, but it is still learning. Do not expect him to catch on to everything right away. A dog is often only as good as his teacher. It is up to you to be consistent and to time your clicks and mark behavior so your dog knows what you want.

Once you have learned the basics of clicker training, you can teach your dog basic obedience, tricks, and other behaviors. Clicker training is also excellent for handling behavior problems. It is a good approach to learning in general.

CASE STUDY: ROBIN AND DOG TRAINING

Robin Anderson
Grampian Labradors, reg.
Seekonk, Massachusetts

Robin Anderson has been deeply involved with Labrador retrievers for years. She trains them for obedience, conformation breed shows, and for hunting. She knows the importance of good communication.

"When you work as a team on a task with a dog, both the human and the dog learn how to get their needs met," Robin says. "It is mutually satisfying for both the human and the dog when both understand the task and how to get it accomplished. The human is proud of the dog and feels good about training/owning it. The dog wants to please in all ways. When the dog is successful in understanding what the trainer wants, the dog is happy and more confident in the learning process. This makes the dog more willing the next time there is a training session, and the dog can learn more easily."

Robin says that dogs can respond to many kinds of communication but people have to learn to interpret a dog's body language. "I think it all works in tandem. Most dogs will respond to all types of communication, but some dogs respond better to one over another depending on the individual dog.

Because dogs can't talk per se, I think it's the overall body language we learn to interpret and understand. Some dogs are more vocal than others, but mainly we learn their body language. I think lack of consistency makes communication difficult between dogs and handlers. Find what works with that dog and use it again."

Robin recommends that people find a good mentor for training. "Unless you've had a good mentor in training, and the handler has good dog skills, ANY dog communication can be hard. Get a training mentor you get along with. Two heads are often better than one when trying to interpret dog communication in training. I had a dog I didn't understand. I thought she was dog aggressive. Once I hooked up to the right mentor in training, I learned that she was afraid of other dogs and needed me to build her confidence by becoming her true pack leader. No more nice guy stuff from me. I gave her firm commands, demanded she pay attention to me, and promised I'd protect her from other dogs. I didn't coddle her or accept her aggressive tendencies. She became a good working dog as a result and in her middle years accepted all kinds of other dogs into her life because of my leadership."

According to Robin, food is a great motivator for dogs. "Most dogs respond great to food when training. Anything associated with food can work well to get a point across to a dog. Robin also says that good leadership with your dog is important. "I see this with pet owners all the time. We raise Labradors for all kinds of things: pets, working dogs, hunting dogs. The pet owners love their new puppies so much and fail to give them proper leadership along with the love. I think of Ceasar Milan always telling clients that they need to establish respect from the dog first, and then they can give love. Thus, the new puppy learns that they can do about anything they want and never receive guidance. Before too long the dog is *big* and out of control. Thankfully, we keep in contact with many puppy buyers and help them train their dogs before this happens or are able to help correct a situation before it's out of control. I got a two-year-old Labrador back because the family couldn't afford to keep her any more. The poor dog had never been taught to climb stairs for fear of ruining her joints. I had to be *very* firm and use the Ceasar method to teach her stairs on lead. It took a week of my being insistent she'd go up and down stairs. Once she learned she wasn't going to die, she was very proud and happy with herself. She also had never been taught to allow her toenails to be groomed with either clippers or a Dremel®. The first few times we used the Dremel® the dog screamed, kicked, and fought two adults to get us to stop the grooming. We persisted, she didn't die, and after a few times of this behavior that we didn't back off from, she learned she had to submit to grooming and came to enjoy it. Both of these training incidents resulted in love and cookies once she learned she had to obey and submit to the leadership. This dog is now in a hunting home with a man who loves her enthusiastic energy. The dog loves to learn new things and doesn't exhibit any more fear when presented with something new. She's got confidence in herself and respects her new handler/owner."

Choosing a Training Method for Your Dog

Dogs are individuals, just as people are. Some dogs respond better to certain kinds of training. Some owners also have a better grasp of one kind of training. There are more than 400 breeds of dogs in the world, along with countless mixed breeds, designer dogs, and plain mutts. The same method of training will not work for every dog.

Breeds of dogs were bred for different purposes, and they have different temperaments. Terriers can be feisty and bold, for example. Sporting dogs are often energetic but soft natured and eager to please their owners. Hounds can be independent and willing to make their own decisions. That is why different training methods can produce different results with different dogs. It is not necessarily a question of intelligence. A dog might be highly intelligent, but if you are using a training method that is inappropriate for him, he might learn slowly or not at all.

Your dog's individual personality and temperament will determine how he responds to different training methods. Most dogs respond well to positive reinforcement training using praise and rewards. Clicker training is popular now. If you plan to sign up for a training class, it is easy to find clicker training classes, and most dogs will do well with this kind of training. However, do not feel compelled to take a clicker training class. Traditional dog training classes are still taught, and they can be a good choice for some dogs.

If you have one of the breeds commonly rated as extremely intelligent, such as a border collie, poodle (all sizes), German shepherd, golden retriever, Doberman pinscher, Shetland sheepdog, Labrador retriever, papillon, rottweiler, or the Australian  cattle dog (per Stanley Coren and his book *The Intelligence of Dogs*), your dog is probably easy to train and will respond quickly to positive reinforcement. However, if you have a breed that is less interested in pleasing, or less food-motivated, positive reinforcement might not be the best choice for your dog. This is especially true if you have a dog that tends to be hardheaded and stubborn. In that case, traditional dog training or a mixture of methods might work better. You might need to be creative when working with your dog and use a combination of positive reinforcement exercises, traditional dog training methods, and simple dog training techniques.

Training Specific Breeds

There are more than 400 recognized breeds of dog in the world today, and all of them exist because of human selective breeding. Many of these breeds date back millennia. The Afghan hound, the Akita Inu, the Alaskan malamute, the basenji, the chow chow, the Lhasa apso, the Pekingese, the shar-pei, the saluki, the Samoyed, the Shiba Inu, the shih tzu, the Siberian Husky, and the Tibetan terrier were found through DNA testing to be the oldest breeds among 85 AKC breeds tested; but other breeds might be just as old.

In the United States, the American Kennel Club® divides dogs into seven categories or groups: sporting, hound, working, terrier, toy, non-sporting, and herding. These groups are based on the dogs' work or function, or the work they did at one time. Most dogs today are kept as pets, but not long ago nearly all dogs had jobs. Some dogs still work today, though they might not do their original job. Dogs are highly adaptable, and their intelligence is such that many breeds have taken on new roles. For example, the Labrador retriever is often identified as a hunting dog or family pet, but they also excel as search and rescue dogs and explosives dogs because of their outstanding noses, in addition to their work as assistance dogs.

If you have a dog from one of these groups, it will definitely be easier to train your dog to do his traditional work. For instance, beagles are often eager to follow the trail of any rabbit or small creature they encounter, and training them to hunt rabbits is much easier that it would be to train some other breeds. They have the nose and the predisposition to want to hunt them. A sight hound such as the saluki is "hardwired" to go after prey.

They have the physical traits and the mental abilities needed to be good at their job. In the same way, it is easy to teach water dogs such as the Newfoundland to swim and even to rescue people. These are natural abilities for them.

Dogs have abilities because of centuries of selective breeding. Dogs of beagle type that were good at hunting rabbits were constantly selected and bred to produce better beagles. The same is true with all of the other breeds. This is how dog breeds have been developed all the way back to the time when humans first domesticated the dog. Perhaps they started by selecting wolf-dogs that could help them with hunting. These dogs would become our hounds and sporting dogs. They selected dogs that could guard flocks. These dogs would become herding dogs. They selected dogs that could pull carts and guard the home, and these dogs became the working dogs. And so on as they kept finding dogs to fill every job they needed a dog to do, including dogs to be lapdogs. So, our dogs today can learn to do these jobs easily because they have been chosen to do them from the beginning.

However, just because a dog is good at hunting or water rescues or search and rescue, it does not mean it is hard for him to learn to be a good family pet. All dogs have been selected for thousands of years for traits that make them welcome in our homes. Additionally, every dog is an individual. Plus, all of the breeds in the world have different temperaments and abilities. Some hounds are easier than others to train; the same is true with herding dogs or terriers or the other breeds. Fortunately, not everyone wants the same kind of dog, so there is a dog for everyone.

If you are thinking of getting a dog, the best thing you can do is to research the breeds that interest you and find out about their temperaments, what they are like with children, their grooming needs, how big they get, how much exercise they need, and their health information. Make sure you choose the right dog for you.

You can teach your dog to sit in many different ways. With positive reinforcement, you can click when your dog sits and reward him, then repeat this again until your dog catches on. This can take some time with some dogs. With traditional dog training, you can teach your dog to sit by pushing down on his hips and releasing pressure when he is in the sitting position. Then there is the practical approach, which is not really part of any "method." With your dog standing, you can hold a treat over his nose. Slowly move the treat backward over your dog's head. Your dog should lower his hips into a sitting position. Then give your dog the treat. This approach does involve some positive reinforcement, but it does not use a clicker. You are luring your dog into position to do what you want him to do.

Sometimes training is just about being creative and finding ways to communicate what you want to your dog.

The training you do with your dog can improve your relationship in every way. Training helps you and your dog become more aware of each other physically, mentally, and emotionally. Training takes regular practice and spending time with your dog, as you work toward common goals. You and your dog have to work on your communication skills to achieve success, no matter which training method you use. You will be trying to teach your dog specific commands and what you want him to learn while your dog is trying to comprehend what you are trying to teach him. The more you and your dog work at your training, the more in tune you will be with your communication.

Before any training can take place, dogs need to learn how to live in human society. They need to know the rules of living in the human world. Socialization forms the basis of all dog training and, indeed, teaches a dog to have good manners so he can live happily in the home. In the next chapter, we will look at dog training and the theories behind training your puppy or adult dog.

CASE STUDY: DONNA AND DOG TRAINING

Donna Bost
Denver, North Carolina

I teach mostly obedience training. In proper training, the owner learns to listen to what the dog needs for the most efficient learning environment. The dog has a better understanding of what you expect of them in all life situations.

I find that dogs rely more on body language and some facial expressions. They seem to catch on to sign language very quickly. Owners seem to like words, and they expect their dogs to know English when the owner does not try to teach the dog to understand. Putting an action with a word is the hardest communication issue for dogs to understand. The correct action and rewards are the easiest communication issues for dogs to understand.

To help your dog understand, do not repeat a word over and over....... sit, sit, sit.......say the word one time and if the dog does not get it, help him. Work in short positive sessions. Do not get upset with your dog. They want to please you, and if they understand what you want, they will give it, happily.

Dogs are naturally happy and willing workers, but owners get upset when the dog does not respond to their requests and break the dog down. Then the dog just goes through the motions to please but is not having a good time. Training should be fun for both parties. Keep it happy and uplifting and you will both have a good time.

CHAPTER FIVE

Obedience Training

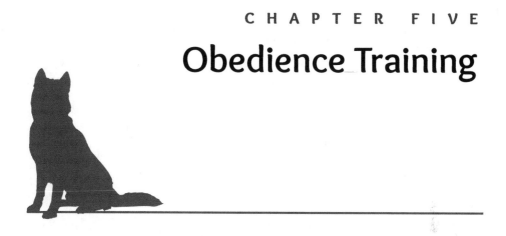

All dogs can benefit from obedience training. It makes your dog a better pet and a better member of the community. Additionally, training your dog is an excellent way to improve your communication with your dog.

Reasons You Should Train Your Dog

There are many reasons to train your dog. Some of the reasons benefit you, and some of them benefit your dog, but you will both of you be better off with training.

1. Many dogs lose their homes each year because of behavior problems, especially puppies and young adults. If they are not easily housetrained, if they jump up on people or if the dog barks too much, owners might decide to get rid of the dog by taking him to the local animal shelter. Often, these dogs are never adopted. With just a little training, puppies and young adult dogs can usually overcome these behavior problems and keep their homes.

2. Dogs that are trained are more responsive to their owners. They watch and listen for commands. They focus on their owners and are less easily distracted. Dogs and owners become more attuned to each other, and owners find that they love to spend time with their dogs. Plus, the more you teach your dog, the more he is capable of learning.

3. Dogs can have lots of fun with training, especially using positive reinforcement. The dog is being rewarded for doing something that he enjoys doing — pleasing the owner. The owner enjoys success with training the dog. Training is rewarding for the dog and the owner.

4. Training is good way to get to know your dog better. You have a common goal. It is a good way to get closer to your dog and understand how his mind works. You are not just teacher and student. You are best friends.

5. You can improve your relationship with your dog through training. The more you work together and the more your dog learns, the closer your bond will grow. Your dog will become better at understanding you, and you will understand him better, too.

6. Once you have mastered basic obedience training, you can move on to more advanced training such as rally, agility, flyball, and other things that you and your dog would enjoy doing together. All of these activities rely on dogs and owners having a close relationship built via training.

7. Everyone likes a well-trained dog. Businesses that cater to pets such as veterinarians, groomers, doggie day cares, and others will welcome your dog if he is well trained.

8. Training can save your dog's life. The dog that comes when called will not run out in front of a car. The dog that does not rush through the door to escape will not become lost or injured. These situations show how training can save your dog from disaster.

How Training Your Dog Improves Your Communication

Training your dog requires you spend time together with a common goal. No matter which training method you are using, in order to succeed, you will need to focus on basic lessons. Each lesson should have goals that you can articulate to yourself, such as teaching your dog to sit, to lie down, or to walk on a loose leash. Your mission with each lesson will be to communicate this goal

to your dog. This means that good communication will be essential to both of you. Most of the time when a dog does not do what you want him to do, it is because he is confused or does not understand what you want him to do. This is usually due to a failure in communication on your part.

The more you train with your dog, the better you will become at conveying to your dog what you want him to do. Your dog also will become better at understanding how you communicate your wishes to him. Your communication with your dog will improve, and training will become easier. However, it does take practice and work. You must train regularly.

Daily training is best. If you only train once a week, your dog will not progress. Most dogs have short attention spans, so it is better to train for 15 to 20 minutes per session, two or three times per day, instead of trying to train in one long marathon session if you can set your own training times. (If you are taking a training class the lessons probably will be longer and will occur once or twice per week.) You also should try to keep things fun for your dog. Dogs generally learn best if they are having a good time and you keep the training more like play.

Training is like any skill. The training you do with your dog will improve the more you practice it, and so will your communication. Owners and dogs that train often can develop a close bond. Dogs often seem to almost read their owners' minds. In actuality, the dogs have been training with their owners so much that they can read the tiniest clues in their owners' faces or movements and know what is coming next. You, too, can achieve this level of communication with your dog through training if you work hard with your dog.

CASE STUDY: JANI AND HER DOGS

Jani Wolstenholme
Newport, Rhode Island

How many dogs do you have?

I have had dogs for 35 years. I currently have two.

Some of the everyday words and phrases my dogs know are "walk," "eat," "go for a ride," "cookies," "crate," "leave it," "off," "sit," "down," "go lay down," squirrel," and "birds."

When my male's water dish is either low or empty, he repeatedly will come to me, bark, and then run to the dish. He also runs to the front door when someone pulls into the driveway, whining, even if he doesn't know who it is.

One time in particular, my dog and I had an obvious miscommunication. I was reading in my bedroom when he left the room. He barked a few times, but I told him to be quiet. I heard water running and thought a pipe had burst. He was in the bathroom and had turned the water on in the sink. I never taught him that; he learned evidently from watching me. He was out of water downstairs!

As far as improving my communication with dogs, I'd like to understand the dog I got as a 6-year-old who was mostly raised a kennel dog and doesn't understand either my obedience commands or everyday language (off, leave it, etc.). Or I'm not using the right words with her. Recently, I've been taking her to a beginner's obedience class. I'm still working on understanding her.

To others trying to communicate with your dogs, use the same words all the time so as not to confuse what you mean. Repetition and consistency are important early on. Teach hand signals. I train with food or toys and make everything as fun as possible.

Developing a Language with Your Dog

Basic obedience training is good for all dogs and will help dogs and owners develop a level of shared communication. A dog that knows "sit," "come," "lie down," and other basic commands and that can walk calmly on a leash is a dog with good manners. Any owner can be proud of such a dog. Dogs who have learned these basics are far less likely to have behavior problems. For example, "sit" can be used to solve many behavior issues. If your dog jumps up on people, he is less likely to do so if he is sitting politely as he has been taught. A dog is less likely to bolt out the door into the street if you can put him into a sit-stay before you open the door to visitors. Simply knowing basic commands can do wonders for your dog's behavior and will improve your communication with your dog.

However, your dog needs to know more than obedience commands. He is smart and capable of learning dozens, perhaps a couple of hundred words. Your daily life with your dog, starting when he is a puppy, will go much more smoothly if you teach him what he needs to know. Dogs might not rely on words as much as humans do, but that does not mean they do not need to know some words.

Here is a sample vocabulary for dogs:

Good	Crate	Keys
Yes	Bed	Mine
No	Outside	Bath
Naughty	Out	Groomed
Food	Door	Table
Breakfast	Walk	Brush
Hungry	Potty	Nails
Dinner	Leash	Paw
Eat	Collar	Ears
Bedtime	Ride	Teeth

This is just a sample of words for basic things such as walking your dog, feeding him, going for a ride, and being groomed. These are not a lot of words for a dog to understand. Your dog probably knows many more. Dogs pick up words all the time, based on context. They probably do not follow entire sentences, but they notice key words that are used often.

Be careful what you teach your dog. There is an old joke that a dog thinks his name is "Dammit, Rex." In some cases, you might have to start spelling words, such as B-A-T-H, or using a different word so your dog will not know what you are saying.

Deciding to Train at Home or Take a Class

It is up to you whether you train your dog at home or take a class. Puppies and dogs can be successfully trained both ways. In addition to the information provided in this book, DVDs and videos about dog training are available to help you train your dog at home. Many people have trained their own dogs at home, and their dogs would astonish you with their abilities.

Finding classes

You also can go to classes for dog training. You and your dog will work on obedience lessons taught by an instructor. Classes usually meet once or twice a week for six or eight weeks. You can find  classes at a training center, through a pet store, offered by a kennel club, given by a professional trainer, or even through your local animal shelter. Before signing up for any classes, you always should do a little investigating. Make sure the instructor is qualified. Find out what methods they use. If you object to traditional dog training using choke collars, find out if the class uses these methods. And, of course, find out about the costs for the class and other pertinent facts.

If the class seems acceptable to you, it is likely that you and your dog can learn a great deal. Professional instructors are often experts or at least trainers with a lot of experience in training dogs. They can teach you how to train your dog and deal with any problems you are having in class. You still will need to go home and practice what you learn in class.

Choosing an instructor

You might find that you have a choice of trainers and training methods, so you can ask your family and friends if they know a trainer they can recommend. As with any profession, word of mouth and reputation count. If someone has a bad experience with a dog trainer, you should consider that.

In the United States, no laws regulate dog trainers. Anyone can take out an ad and say he or she is a dog trainer. That is why it is important to ask a few questions about the qualifications of the person offering a training class.

Many dog training schools offer classes for people who wish to become dog trainers. Some of them are better than others. If you are looking for a trainer for you and your dog, seek out a trainer who has certification from one of the well-known professional dog training organizations in this country.

The Certification Council for Professional Dog Trainers offers the CPDT-KA designation—Certified Professional Dog Trainer—Knowledge Assessed. This certification indicates that the trainer has at least 300 hours of experience, references from a vet, a client, and a colleague; and has passed an exam testing all aspects of their knowledge about dogs, training, and teaching techniques. CCPDT has professional dog trainers not just in North America but also in Europe, Australia, Japan, and Hong Kong.

The Association of Pet Dog Trainers does not offer certification, but they require certification from one of the following organizations as a prerequisite for membership:

- Certification Council for Professional Dog Trainers
- Animal Behavior Society
- International Association of Animal Behavior Consultants
- International Association for the Study of Animal Behavior
- American College of Veterinary Behaviorists

Most trainers will attend a dog training school and/or apprentice with an expert in the field before being certified. This is necessary because certification requires around 300 hours of experience as a trainer or instructor. Some of this work can be done working with shelter animals.

Good dog training schools also should offer the prospective trainer classes in dog behavior, anatomy, genetics, diseases, history of dog training, dog psychology, and different approaches to training. Prospective trainers also will need to learn how to work with clients and handle different situations with different dogs.

When you choose a dog trainer, it is perfectly acceptable to ask about their certification and what kind of training and experience they have had. You are choosing someone to work with you and your dog, so it is important for you to choose wisely.

You might find a trainer who connects well with you and your dog. On the other hand, you might have a trainer who, for whatever reason, is not a good "fit" for you and your dog. If you are not making the kind of progress you hope for and you are doing the work, you might need to change trainers. Do not give up on training because you have a trainer who is not the best choice for you. Choosing a different trainer might make a world of difference. Someone who presents the same information in a different way might be able to make a big difference to you and your dog.

Not all good trainers will have certification, but many of the best trainers do. Find out about anyone who will be spending time with your dog and giving you advice. You want to make sure you are receiving good advice before you follow it.

Training your dog at home

When training at home, you have to be consistent with your dog. Training can fail when owners 1) stop and start training; and 2) allow their dogs to be inconsistent about obeying commands.

When training at home, you should train in two short sessions per day. Keep the sessions about 15 to 20 minutes long. If they are longer than that, your dog will become bored, especially if you have a puppy. Two short, interesting lessons will be more productive than one long, boring lesson.

Whether you are training at home or practicing following a class, require your dog to complete the commands you are working on. Commands like "sit" and "come" are easy to teach. Training can fail when an owner does not make the dog follow through with the exercises. For example, if you are teaching your dog to sit and he lies down instead, he is not completing the exercise. You should not accept this response. Be consistent with the commands you give your dog and the responses that you accept from him. If you do this during all of your training sessions, your dog will learn more quickly.

Training at home is a good choice for many owners. All dogs need to learn some basic obedience lessons, even if it is only some good manners. You might not have the money to invest in formal training with an instructor, but you can still teach your dog what he needs to learn.

You can teach your dog at home the same things he would learn in a formal training class such as "sit," "come," "lie down," "stay," and to walk on a loose leash. Dogs that know these basic commands will be better behaved at home and in public. For example, a dog that knows the sit command will not jump on people. You can teach him to sit politely when visitors come to your home instead of trying to jump on them or bolt out the door. Learning one command can help improve your dog's behavior.

If you are training your dog at home using positive reinforcement techniques, you will need a flat buckle collar and a leash that is about six feet long. Most people use a nylon collar and leash. They are durable and inexpensive. You also will need a bait bag or pouch of some kind to hold treats. This does not need to be expensive either. You can use a fanny pack or a sandwich bag. For food rewards, you will need small treats so your dog will not fill up on them. You can use sliced hot dog bits, pieces of cheese, pieces of dog food, or training treats that you buy at the pet store. You do not need to spend a lot of money on any of these things.

If you will be using clicker training to train your dog, you will need a couple of clickers. It is a good idea to get one plus a spare in case you lose one or it breaks. They are inexpensive and easy to find. You can buy them at your local pet store or online. They cost $2 to $3 each, or you can buy several for a bulk price on eBay. Some clickers come with wristbands so you can keep it handy while you work with your dog.

Whether you train at home or you take a class, how much and how fast your dog learns will depend on how much you work with him. If you only train for five minutes before class, your dog is not going to learn much. On the other hand, if you train steadily each day, your dog will learn a lot and remember what you work on together. How much your dog learns is up to you and the effort you put into the training.

Teaching Your Dog Basic Obedience Commands

If you have a puppy, you can begin teaching him basic obedience commands as early as about 8 weeks old. Keep your lessons short, and make sure they are fun. Use lots of praise with puppies. The more like a game the training is, the better. For adult dogs, no dog is too old to learn. You can teach an old dog new tricks. If you have a rescue dog or you have adopted a dog and you do not know his background, it is possible that he already knows some commands, so try out a few basic commands first to see if he knows some. You might be surprised to find he already knows a little obedience.

Sit and lie down

If your puppy is not used to wearing a collar yet, put the collar on him and let him wear it in the house for a while. Most puppies get used to a collar quickly, though he might paw at it at first. Attach the leash to the collar and let him drag it around for a few minutes. Be sure to stand close by so he does not catch the leash on anything. You do not want him to choke himself or knock something over on top of himself. You just  want him to get used to the feeling of something pulling on the collar. Then you can remove the leash or the leash and the collar.

When you are working on your puppy's training, work in an open area that is free of distractions. Do *not* let your puppy off leash unless you are in an enclosed area, such as your own backyard. You do not want to spend the next hour chasing your puppy. Remember that it is not safe to allow your puppy off leash even if you have been practicing the "come" command. It will take a great deal of practice before your puppy is reliable, and even then, be careful about allowing your puppy off leash.

Your puppy will be able to learn most basic obedience commands by the time he is 6 months old, but it will take regular practice to help him remember them. His performance might be a little hit or miss in the beginning, so do not expect perfection. Remember that he is just a puppy. Keep things fun for him when training, and you will soon have a well-trained dog.

It is fairly easy to teach a puppy to sit. You can start by saying "sit" each time your puppy sits on his own. Give him a treat if you have one. Your puppy will make the connection. Or, you can lure your puppy into a sitting position by holding a treat over his head when he is standing and gradually moving the treat backward until he is sitting. Keep saying "sit," and give him the treat when he is sitting. Remember to praise him. You can do the same thing with "lie down." Use a treat to lure him into lying down from the sitting position.

You also can teach your puppy to sit by using the clicker. In this case, be prepared ahead of time by having some small treats in a pouch or in your pocket. Have the clicker with you. In one scenario, when your puppy sits on his own, you should immediately click the clicker and give him a treat. Do this each time he sits on his own in order to "shape" his behavior, to use a conditioning term. Your puppy will start to make the connection between the behavior, the clicking, and treats.

In a second scenario, you can set the scene for your puppy. With your puppy sitting or standing in front of you, toss a treat on the floor for him to get that is slightly out of his reach so he has to get up to get it. Once he gets up to get the treat and returns to sit down, click the clicker and reward him with another treat. Then toss another treat so he has to get up and get it. When he sits down again, click and treat. Keep doing this until he catches on and learns to sit when you use the "sit" command. Make sure your treats are tiny because this can take a lot of treats.

Another way to teach your puppy to sit is by gently pushing down on his hindquarters and then releasing them when he is in the sitting position. Be sure to praise him for sitting and give him a reward. Make sure that you do not push too hard. You do not want to cause any kind of hip injury when you push on your puppy's hips.

You can also teach your puppy to lie down by gently pulling his front legs forward when he is in the sitting position and using the "lie down" command. Praise and reward him.

Come

If you want to learn how to train your dog to come, it is not too difficult. Teaching your dog to come when called is one of the most important lessons that your dog can learn. Coming when called literally can save your dog's life. If you are walking your dog and the leash breaks or if your dog gets out of the

house or yard, then having your dog come when called could keep him from running in front of a car. It could keep him from being killed, injured, or lost.

To teach your dog to come, you will need a long cord or rope to attach to his collar. A cord or rope that is 15 to 20 feet long is about the right length for most dogs. Have some dog training treats and one of your dog's favorite toys. The treats can be anything that your dog really likes, such as cheese, cut up hot dog bits, pieces of chicken, or kibble. It just needs to be something that your dog always will be eager to eat. The pieces should be medium-sized. When your dog comes to you, he should feel as though he has received a good reward, but you do not want him to fill up too quickly.

To teach your dog to come when called, attach the cord or rope to your dog's collar and put the collar on your dog. Then walk your dog in your backyard or somewhere else where you will be largely free of distractions. You can teach your dog to come in a park as long as there are not too many other things going on around you.

Once your dog is wearing the collar with the cord attached and you are in the yard, let your dog wander around and forget about the cord. Let him sniff things and become interested in the grass or trees. After your dog is a few yards away from you, lean down and say your dog's name and "Come!" Your dog will not have any idea what this means, of course, but tug a little on the collar and show him his favorite toy. Use a high-pitched happy voice and make it sound like fun to come to you. Do not drag your dog to you. If he starts toward you and stops, you can tug gently on the cord again and repeat, "Come!" Keep waving the toy and showing him that it is fun. Your dog should come to you in just a few seconds. As soon as your dog comes to you, give him a treat, pet him and fuss over him, and let him play with the toy. Act like coming to you when you call him is the greatest thing he ever did in his life. Remember that learning this lesson can save your dog's life, so you should really celebrate with him.

As soon as you and your dog are finished celebrating this first success, let your dog start wandering around the yard again until he has forgotten the cord. Then repeat the exercise again. Call your dog, say, "Come!" Wiggle the toy, tug the cord, and really celebrate when your dog comes to you.

If you repeat this lesson several times each day, your dog will learn to come reliably when you call him If your dog is still reluctant to come when you call him, try turning and trotting away from him. One of the best ways to get a dog to come is to run away from him. Dogs love to chase things, and your dog will chase you if you run from him.

It will take some time before you can trust your dog to come to you without the cord. Always give this lesson in an enclosed area in case your dog gets away from you, especially when you start trying to do it without the cord. Before you start trying to teach your dog to come to you without the cord, you can take your dog to a friend's house and try getting your dog to come to you with the cord there. You can try the lesson when there are more distractions. Use your imagination and make the test more difficult for your dog. The ultimate test will be if your dog ever gets away from you in public and you have to rely on him to come when you call him. Ideally, that will never happen.

Teaching your dog to come is a relatively easy lesson to teach, but it takes a great deal of practice and proofing before a dog is perfect at it. Keep practicing this lesson throughout your dog's life.

Walk on a loose leash

Owners often complain that their dog pulls on the leash, which can make it hard to take the dog for a walk or go anywhere. You can teach your puppy to walk on a loose leash so you will not have a problem with him pulling you wherever you go. Even if you have an adult dog, you can correct pulling behavior by teaching your dog to walk on a loose leash.

You can practice this lesson in your backyard, in a park, or any place where you will have space to walk with your puppy or dog. The easiest way to teach your puppy or dog to walk on a loose leash is by making yourself a "tree" when he begins to pull on the leash. In other words, when your dog starts to pull, you should freeze and stop moving. Do not budge. Become "tree-like." It will only take a few seconds for your puppy or dog to realize that you are not moving, and he has come to the end of the leash. At this point, your dog will turn around, look at you, and then come back to you. He probably will give you a look as if to say, "Hey, let's go." When your puppy or dog returns to you, you can move forward again. Repeat this pattern each time your puppy or dog begins to pull on the leash. Your dog will soon figure out that if he wants to go anywhere, he will need to stay next to you and stop pulling.

If your dog continues to pull on the leash, despite freezing in place when he pulls, you can try taking your dog on some zigzag walks. You will need a larger area for this method, and it must be a place that is unfamiliar to your dog so he has to watch you to see where you are going. Set out walking with your puppy or dog and walk for ten or 15 seconds in any direction. Then change direction. It does not matter which direction you go. The important thing is to change direction and keep your dog guessing. Walk in that direction for another ten or 15 seconds and change direction again. Keep this up for five or ten minutes. Your dog will not be able to pull on the leash because he will have no idea which way you are going to go next. You probably will not be able to do this lesson for more than about ten minutes because it is mentally tiring, even though you do not cover much ground. However, it teaches your dog to pay attention to you, and dogs learn to stop pulling on the leash.

Heel

Your puppy also should learn to heel when you train him. This means that your puppy will walk calmly beside you without pulling on the leash. It is good to practice this exercise in a wide-open area with few distractions. The exercise will involve lots of walking. If your puppy starts pulling, then you will stop. Your puppy will learn that if he wants to move forward, he will need to walk politely. You can emphasize this lesson by walking in different directions and changing directions frequently to keep your puppy guessing. That way, he will have to watch you to see what you are going to do. He cannot pull and run off if he does not know where you are going. A correct heel includes teaching your puppy to sit politely by your left knee when you stop walking. Heeling is different than walking on a loose leash because it requires more control and precision from the dog, but it can be taught much the same way. In both cases, the puppy or dog should not pull on the lead.

You can make heeling fun for your puppy or dog by using a large spoon heaped with peanut butter. You can also use cream cheese or Cheez Whiz®. Stand with your dog sitting by your left knee. Have your dog's collar and leash on to start training. You can remove the leash later after your dog becomes good at heeling. Hold a large spoon filled with a creamy treat in your left hand. Lower the spoon momentarily so your dog can lick it and then raise it. Say, "heel," and set off walking. If your dog begins to lag behind or pull ahead, lower the spoon for a moment to remind your dog of the treat. When you stop walking, give your dog the "sit" command, and let him lick the spoon for a moment. Your dog should begin to sit on his own when you stop walking. Continue to practice heeling until your dog is right by your side whenever you walk.

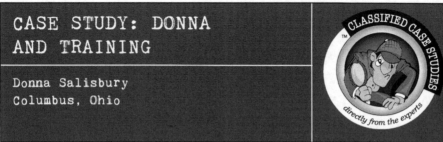

CASE STUDY: DONNA AND TRAINING

Donna Salisbury
Columbus, Ohio

Donna Salisbury has had dogs for 46 years. She currently has 4 dogs. She says that she is usually aware of her dogs' body language and some-times knows what they want when they look at her. She recognizes her dogs' barks, depending on the context.

Donna's dogs know a lot of different words such as: "walk," "car ride," "brush," "treat," "dinner," "breakfast," "carrots," "green beans," "sit," "down," "kick it," "give me five," "other side," "get around," "jump," "chair," "couch," "place," "bath," "touch it," "feet," "ball," "off," and "baby."

Donna does a lot of things to improve communication with her dogs. She does agility training, takes obedience classes, and plays games with her dogs. She says that her communication with her dogs has improved since she started doing this kind of training.

According to Donna, one of the things she would like to improve about her communication with her dogs is to have more time to understand "dogology."

Asked if she has any advice for others about communicating with their dogs, Donna said that people should try to build a solid foundational relationship with their dogs.

Sit-stay

Your puppy's training should also include the "sit and stay" command. With this command, your puppy learns that he should stay in place when you tell him to. You will start by telling him to stay (in the sitting position) while you are quite close, and then you gradually will increase the distance that you move away from him. It does take some time for the puppy to learn the difference between "sit" and "stay." If your puppy hops up and runs to you, take him back to the sitting position and give him the stay command again. Do not praise him for coming to you without permission but do not punish him either. He should stay in the sit-stay position until you release him with a word like "OK!" Do not expect him to sit-stay for very long at first. You should praise and reward your puppy when you release him.

Stand

Your puppy also should learn to "stand." This is an important lesson so your puppy knows how to stand calmly for examination at the vet or at a pet groomer. With your puppy standing, you can talk calmly to him, give him a treat, and repeat the "stand" command. Have a friend come over to pet your puppy and run his hands

over your puppy's body so your puppy will get used to having someone examine him. Have someone pick up his paws and brush him to simulate a trip to the groomer.

Working on leash and off leash

Whether you are working with a puppy or an adult dog, it is usually advisable to work on leash in an enclosed area when you are introducing a new lesson. Choose a place free of distractions. You want to have as much control over the situation and your dog as possible when you are teaching your dog something new. You would not want your dog to chase after a squirrel when you are trying to teach him to come to you.

It is not always necessary to have a collar and leash on your puppy or dog if you are training in your living room. If you are teaching your puppy to sit in a room in your house, for example, you do not have to have a collar on him. He is already in a confined area, and you do not need to attach a leash to a collar for this lesson. However, you should maintain control of the area where you will be training. The fewer distractions, the better.

Once your puppy or dog has mastered the commands you are teaching him on leash, you can begin practicing them off leash. You still should work in an enclosed area at this time to maintain control over your dog. For example, if you are practicing heeling with your dog off leash, it is important to be absolutely certain your dog is heeling reliably at your side before you begin practicing in an open area. Before you take your dog to a park or a place where your dog could get away from you, you should "proof" your dog by taking him places to practice where there will be distractions so you can be sure that he will obey you off leash. You can take him to a friend's yard, perhaps, where he might be tempted to ignore your commands.

Working with your dog off leash in public should be the final step in your training. It can take a long time to reach this point with some commands, such as coming when called. Practice is essential.

The importance of regular practice

No matter what you are trying to teach your dog, it is important to train regularly. You might have one wonderful lesson with your puppy or dog in which he seems to catch on and understand what you are communicating to him. However, if you do not repeat the lesson fairly soon afterward, your dog likely will forget it. Most obedience commands require quite a few repetitions for a dog to be able to perform them reliably on command. Even positive reinforcement training and clicker training will need to be done with lots of repetitions. Your dog is learning. It is not mindless repetition. You often can see a dog making connections and figuring things out for himself. But it does take practice to give your dog time to make the connections between what you are having him do and what you want him to learn.

Key Things to Remember about Training Your Dog

Clear communication is essential for successful dog training. That means:

- Make your timing perfect, including your praise and rewards.
- Be consistent with your expectations.
- Praise generously.
- Firmness is important but you must also be fair.

As you work with your dog, remember these key points:

- There is never any reason to physically harm a dog.
- If you are angry, do not train.
- Be positive when you are training and find a way to end your lessons on a good note, even if you have to go back and do something easy the dog already knows.

You also can improve your training success by making sure your dog is in optimum physical condition. If your dog has any nagging health problems, take him to the veterinarian before starting training. It will be easier for your dog to focus and learn if he feels good.

You dog also needs mental stimulation. If your dog is bored or unhappy, he will be more likely to exhibit behavior problems. Provide toys and play time for your dog. Spend quality time with your dog.

Socialization is the basis for a happy, confident dog. A well-socialized dog will have better communication skills and will get along better with other dogs and with people. These dogs also will learn better.

Choose the best training method for your dog's temperament and personality. You are your dog's trainer, so it is up to you to make the best training decisions for him.

The Most Common Dog Training Mistakes

Although training your dog seems like it should be easy, some common mistakes can undermine your efforts. Some of these mistakes occur in training, and others are related to dog care.

One mistake that often causes problems in dog training occurs when dogs do not get enough exercise. If your dog is home all day and only gets to spend a little time in the backyard, he might not be getting enough exercise, especially if he is a young dog. When you take this dog to a training class or work with him at home, he might have trouble focusing. He has lots of energy, and he is excited. He cannot concentrate on learning to sit. If your dog is excited and frisky, take him for a good run before you start training. Spend some time playing with him for a few minutes before your lessons. Dogs who get plenty of exercise are also much less likely to get into trouble or develop behavior problems.

In addition to lack of exercise, many dogs are eating premium foods with extremely high levels of protein and which are high in calories. Premium foods and good quality protein are both  beneficial but eating a diet suitable for a canine athlete is not necessarily a good thing, especially for a dog that is not getting a lot of activity. Your dog will be better off if you feed him a diet that is suitable for his current activity level, and he will be less likely to become obese. Look for foods that are made for your dog's life stage such as puppy food, maintenance, or foods that are approved for all-life-stages. These foods have been formulated for a dog's nutritional needs at each stage of life. Choose foods with good quality ingredients but do not overfeed your dog or leave food sitting out all day. Measure how much you feed your dog and monitor how much he eats. Leave food down for ten to 15 minutes, and then remove it. Keep your dog at a healthy weight; he should not be chubby or fat. Some foods are dense in calories, so you do not have to feed much food. You can find more information on combating pet weight gain at the Association for Pet Obesity Prevention at **www.petobesityprevention.com**.

If your dog is eating too many calories, is not getting enough exercise, or has more energy than he can constructively use, you are likely to have training problems.

Other possible training problems include accidentally rewarding bad behavior. For example, it can be tempting to soothe a puppy when he is having a bad time, such as during crate training. However, if you pet a puppy that is throwing a fit, you are on your way to having a brat. Likewise, do not pet a dog that jumps up on you, or he will continue to do it. In some cases, the best thing you can do is to ignore bad behavior. If you pay attention to the behavior at all, even to scold the dog, you will be giving the dog attention, and that is what he wants. *More information on correcting for jumping up will be covered in the next chapter.*

Sometimes people also have training problems because they do not know simple dog management techniques. For instance, puppies chew. They will chew anything they can find. There are two ways to deal with puppies that chew: 1) Puppy proof your house; and 2) give them their own things to chew on. You cannot train a puppy not to chew. So hide your remotes, shoes, and everything else you value until your puppy stops chewing. And provide him with lots of acceptable things to chew on so he will be less tempted to chew on your things. This same principle is true for many other dog problems. If your dog is doing something that he should not do, find a way to keep him from doing it. This is often easier than trying to train him, and it produces the same result. For example, if your dog chews on your furniture, you can spend $20 on toys and bitter apple spray, and it will save your $1,500 sofa. This is a management technique. *You will learn more about bitter apply spray in the next chapter.*

Other training problems include bad timing and inconsistency. These things will confuse your dog. If you time your praise or reinforcement incorrectly, your dog will not know what you want. If you click and treat at the wrong time, you are sending the wrong message.

Everyone has a bad training session sometimes. When you are having one, end the lesson before you convey any irritation to your dog. Do not keep going or try to get your dog to do "just one more thing." If your dog is having a problem with a new lesson, then go back and end the lesson by doing something that your dog knows so you can both feel good. The next lesson will go better when you are in a better frame of mind.

Dogs are highly intuitive, and they can sense our feelings. If you are angry or upset when you are training, your dog will know it. Do not train when you are in a bad mood. The lesson probably will not go well. Try to bring a calm, relaxed attitude to your training sessions. Be cheerful and positive when you train your dog. Your lessons together should be a pleasant experience for both of you. This will make your dog more eager to learn.

Do not rush your dog during training. Dogs are capable of learning amazing skills, but they must learn one step at a time. Do not try to skip steps. Move at a comfortable pace for your dog. If you skip steps, you will have to go back and let your dog relearn them later, so take your time.

Remember to praise and reward your dog. Your dog loves to please you, but it is always nice to be appreciated. He is your partner; so let him know he is doing a good job.

CHAPTER SIX

Behavior Problems
of Puppies

Puppies can be irresistible. Male, female, big, small, puppies are cute, and humans seem to be hardwired to want to pick them up and cuddle them. Puppies are happy to oblige any human who wants to pet and play with them. It seems like a match made in heaven. However, puppies do need to be trained. The cute little ball of fur will not stay cute and small forever. Soon, he will turn into a full-grown dog, and his antics might not seem so cute.

Puppy behavior problems are less about serious problems and more about things that puppies need to learn so they will know how they are supposed to behave. Most of these problems are fairly easy to solve if you begin training your puppy when he is young. The longer you let the problem behaviors continue, the harder they are to change.

Your Puppy Has to Learn to Communicate with You

As discussed in the chapter on socialization, puppies are helpless when they are born, and they rely completely on their mothers at first. During their first few weeks, they learn everything about being a dog from their mother and siblings.

Puppies learn to speak "dog" from their mothers and siblings

Many people tend to forget that dogs and puppies are animals. They are not wild animals, but they do rely on their instincts the same way other animals do. Puppies also have  instincts, and these instincts get them started in life. For example, starting almost as soon as their eyes open and they can toddle around, puppies have an instinct to move away from their sleeping area and relieve themselves at a distance from the warm part of the nest. This is not foolproof. Puppies will poop in various places and step in poop, but you can observe puppies moving away from the nest to potty.

Young puppies have instincts to tussle and play-fight with their brothers and sisters. They "attack" and practice hunting and stalking behaviors. They often fight and play too roughly. When this occurs, a puppy's littermates will ignore him temporarily, and no one will play with him. If he refuses to curb his behavior, his mother might nip him. This is how puppies learn bite inhibition so they do not accidentally bite their brothers and sisters too hard when they play.

At this time, puppies also learn to obey their mothers. They learn about pack structure and knowing who is in charge. They have to learn a lot in a short time in the few weeks they are with their mother and littermates.

You have to teach puppies how to communicate with you

When you bring a puppy home, he has not learned how to communicate with you. He might understand that he enjoys petting and playing with you. He might know you feed him, and he might like you, but if you look at him and ask him if he wants to go outside, he has no idea what you are saying or what you mean.

In addition, although he has an instinct that makes him try to avoid soiling his sleeping area, he does not know you consider your entire house to be your "sleeping area." If he is looking for a place to potty, he might avoid your bedroom, for example, but think that it is fine to relieve himself in the laundry room. He is not being dumb. He is using his canine instincts, which are all that he has to go on at this point in his life. It will be up to you to build communication with your puppy and teach him what to do instead.

The same thing is true with other puppy behaviors. Your puppy has learned the basics of bite inhibition regarding his brothers and sisters, but when he plays with you, he will probably have to relearn them. He might bite too hard and play too roughly. You can temporarily ignore him and give him a time-out, the same way his littermates did.

Many puppies enthusiastically jump on people. Puppies tend to jump on each other and on their mother for various reasons (to collect food, to play). You will need to teach your puppy that this behavior is not acceptable when dealing with humans.

Better Communication Can Solve Behavior Problems

If you understand that these behaviors are normal for puppies, it makes it easier to communicate with your puppy and find solutions for them. In many cases, you can preempt a puppy's behavior by reading his body language. For example, puppies are like kids in a lot of ways. If your puppy is out of sight and too quiet, it often means he is doing something he should not be doing. He could be eating your shoes or trying to pull down your drapes. If a puppy saunters back into the room looking pleased with himself, you should check the room from which he just came. He has likely been up to no good. If your puppy takes off running after the cat, you should be in hot pursuit or else the fur could fly. In short, you will need to watch your puppy's behavior and body language like a hawk for the first few weeks and months in order to avoid some common problems.

Housetraining

Start housetraining your puppy from the moment you bring him home. In fact, some puppies might have a head start if they have come from a good breeder. All dogs have an instinct not to soil in the place where they sleep. From the time they can first start toddling around, puppies will start moving away from their sleeping area to relieve themselves. As they get a little older, they will move farther away. If they have the opportunity, as puppies, to use papers or to go outside, they will start to learn some housetraining basics.

When you first bring your puppy home, it is a good idea to stop outside and let your puppy potty. This will give your puppy a chance to see where he is supposed to potty, and it will reduce the likelihood that he will have an accident as soon as he enters the house. The first day in his new house is a very stressful time for your puppy, so he probably will have a few accidents. You will need to be understanding and not lose your cool. If your puppy does have accidents this first day, pick him up, and take him to the spot where you want him to potty, whether it is indoors on papers or outside. Make sure you clean up any spot where your puppy has an accident thoroughly (vinegar and water makes a good cleaner), because your puppy likely will go back there if he smells the odor. You also can buy enzymatic cleaners for this job at the pet store.

Housetraining Basics

As soon as your puppy starts settling in, you can start his housetraining by putting him on a good schedule. Take your puppy outside as soon as you wake up in the morning. Take him outside right after he eats. Take him outside after he plays. Take him outside when he wakes up from a nap. These are all times when young puppies are almost guaranteed to have to potty. You can avoid accidents by hustling your puppy to the place where he is supposed to relieve himself before he has a chance to start wandering around looking for a place to go.

You also will need to learn the subtle signs that your puppy needs to relieve himself. Remember that your puppy is young, and he has not learned how to communicate with you well yet. This means he does not know how to tell you he needs to go out. Watch for the following signs:

- Your puppy starts sniffing the floor.
- He looks for a quiet or hidden place.
- He goes back to the site of a previous accident.
- He looks at the door.
- He looks at you.
- He is too quiet for too long.

If you start noticing these signs, you can take your puppy outside before he has an accident. In time, your puppy will learn how to tell you he needs to go outside. He might bark at you or go sit by the door. He might put a paw on your knee. But at this young age, you will have to guess when he needs to go out. Keep your puppy's collar on him and his leash handy so it will only take a moment to get him outside.

Remember to praise your puppy and give him some treats when he goes to the bathroom outside. You always should let him know he is doing what you want him to do. This will make the housetraining process go much more smoothly.

It does not help to get mad at your puppy or yell at him for making a mistake. Accidents are usually the result of bad timing on your part or missing the signals your puppy is giving you. If you get mad at your puppy for a housetraining mistake, it will only slow his training down.

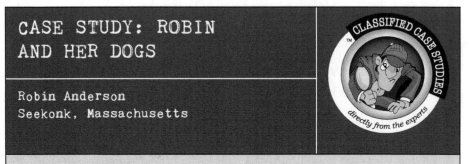

CASE STUDY: ROBIN
AND HER DOGS

Robin Anderson
Seekonk, Massachusetts

I've had dogs all my life, but in my adult life, I've had dogs for about 30 years. I think right now I own or co-own 25 dogs.

I am usually very aware of my dogs' body language, but I can't always tell what my dogs want when they look at me. I know when my dog looks at me, I need to find out what he/she wants by asking questions where I'll get an additional response. A few of my dogs ring a jingle bell at the door to go out. That is VERY clear!

I can't think of one particular time when my dogs and I had an obvious miscommunication, but I learned that one of my dogs hated a certain crate in my van. She was refusing to leave the house to get in the van. She was getting carsick when I put her in a crate behind the driver's seat. She often sat in the crate in a very uncomfortable position. When I finally figured out she was getting sick, I moved her to a crate in the back of the van where she could see out the window, and she stopped getting carsick. When she realized I would give her the preferred crate, she became eager to go for car rides.

My dogs know all the food related words. Labradors are very food motivated. They know all the car words, like "ride," "kennel up," and "car." They know "wanna go?" They know my husband's name. They know some of the names of some toys they regularly play with. They know lots of hunt-related terms: "guns up!" "birdie," "watch," "mark," and "fetch it up." The advanced dogs know more handling terms like "over," "back," "here," and "heel." I honestly think they know many more words than I think they do.

To improve communication with my dogs, I often train with other people in public. We learn in context, and we can learn lots from being with other people who can help solve problems. Puppies always have house training issues at first because we need to learn their signals to go out. Some pups are easy to read. Others are harder to read.

There is always room for improvement. Every dog is a little different, especially between the different breeds. I have Labradors and a French bulldog. Just the difference in bodies makes their body language different. Labs have tails to wag and ears that fly in the wind. French bulldogs are tailless, so it was a while before I could "read" how he was showing me delight and happiness. He also doesn't have the floppy ears that labs have, but he still holds those bat ears in a submissive way and can prick them with interest. The eyes are also different, as is the jaw line. So, I had to learn to understand what the Frenchie's facial expressions were for all his emotions. The other difference is in how they learn. Labs are all about pleasing their people. French bulldogs are more like cats and need different persuasions to get the same results.

Pay attention. They "talk" all the time! It's up to us to learn their language. They know ours!

Paper-Training

If you have a toy dog, a small dog, or you live in an apartment, you might want to consider paper-training your puppy. Many people find paper-training their dog a convenient way to handle housetraining. You can purchase potty training papers at the pet store, which are scented with a chemical to encourage puppies to use them.

If you intend to paper train your puppy, choose a spot that is out of the way and quiet. Place a plastic liner on the floor to prevent urine from leaking through. Then place papers on top of the liner. When your puppy indicates that he needs to relieve himself, you should pick him up and place him on the papers. Make sure you praise him and give him a treat for using the papers.

You also can use products like the Potty Patch® and other products that rely on synthetic grass. The synthetic grass is placed over a tray to catch the urine. You can teach your puppy to potty on the synthetic grass. Cleanup is easy, and the products are easy to disinfect.

No matter what method you use, most puppies can be housetrained in just a few weeks. The important thing to remember is to be persistent and stick to the training. You must keep taking your puppy out at regular times and watch for signals that your puppy needs to go. If you ignore your puppy's signals, you are telling him it is OK to use the bathroom in the house. Do not be surprised if your puppy does not understand what you are trying to teach him. Take him out every single time he looks like he has to go, and he will learn to let you know when he needs to go outside.

Nipping and chewing on people

Have you ever been playing with a puppy and suddenly felt like a chew toy? You know the feeling — when a puppy starts playing too roughly and sinks those sharp little teeth into  you? Many puppies do it. But what can you do to stop it?

First, consider how your puppy has been raised for the first few weeks of his life. As a dog, he has been living with his mother and littermates. When he played with them, it was perfectly all right to use his teeth and nails unless he played too roughly. At that point, his siblings and mother taught him lessons about appropriate behavior. He learned some boundaries, and he learned about bite inhibition.

When you bring your puppy home and you let him chew on you, you are teaching him it is fine to nip and bite you — just the opposite of what he has learned from his mother and littermates. When a few days or weeks go by and it *really* starts to hurt when your puppy bites you, it is too late. You have already taught him that it is OK. If you want to teach him to stop biting you at this point, you have to start over and teach him the same thing that his mother and littermates already taught him. You have to teach your puppy that bite inhibition applies to humans.

When you and your puppy are playing, if your puppy starts playing too roughly and nips you, take a time-out and stop playing with him. Stop all play for at least 30 seconds. Ignore your puppy during this time even if he tries to get you to play. If your puppy calms down and can play calmly, it is fine to resume play. However, if your puppy is still too hyper about playing, continue to ignore him for another five minutes. Give him a real time-out and let him settle down. Ignore him. Do not look at him. After five minutes, you can make friends again.

When your puppy does nip you, let him know it hurt. Give a yelp just as one of his littermates would. Cry out loudly enough to startle him; make sure that he knows he hurt you, and it was not fun. Make it sounds worse than it hurt. Your puppy has no real idea that what he is doing can cause harm, so you are teaching him that there is a connection between his actions and you crying out.

If you continue with these actions each time your puppy plays too roughly or nips you, then your puppy should stop nipping in just a few days.

Do not forget to praise and reward your puppy for playing nicely. You can teach your puppy the kind of play that is desired by petting him and praising him when he is calm.

Always remember that puppies do not bite and nip to be mean. They do not know what they are doing causes pain. When they come to live with us, they probably see us as an extension of their dog family. The only way they know how to play is the same way they played with their canine littermates. It is up to us to teach them better ways to play so no one gets hurt.

And, do not forget that if your puppy is playing with a child in particular, that they always should be supervised. Children under the age of about 5 years old should not be left unattended with dogs. It is easy for play to escalate and get out of hand. Any kind of nipping or biting that involves a child can be serious, so always be on hand to watch when young children and dogs play together. Even a puppy can cause unintentional injury.

Always provide puppies with plenty of their own toys and safe things to chew on. Puppies play hard and often, and they need lots of toys. Provide a wide range of toys to help stimulate a puppy's mental growth. You can find toys that range from simple hard nylon bones to the most creative games. Some toys require a puppy to interact to get the toy to dispense treats or even other toys. Toys today can be quite ingenious. The more they amuse your puppy, the less trouble your puppy will get into in your home. *There is more detailed information about toys in Chapter 2.*

You also can find toys you can use when you are playing with your puppy. Again, make sure that the play does not get too rough. Your puppy needs to learn that whether you are playing one on one or with toys he cannot nip or chew on you. But he should be able to be as rough as he likes with his toys. Some toys might not last long. Some puppies will tear stuffies apart within minutes. Other toys, such as hard rubber Kongs, might last forever. You will discover which toys appeal most to your puppy.

At other times, you might want to play fetch or chase with your puppy in the backyard. That is great, but be careful not to let these games get too wild. Teach children not to run screaming from puppies. Puppies will chase them and quickly become overexcited. Always supervise any play between puppies or dogs and children.

Chewing on furniture and other objects

Puppies chewing on things is one of the behavior problems most often mentioned by dog owners. There are different reasons for chewing depending on the age and situation of your puppy. Regardless of what causes your puppy to chew, you can do some positive things to get him to stop the chewing.

It is not at all unusual for puppies to chew on anything they can put in their mouths. They are a lot like human babies in the sense that they will try to put anything in their mouths and, being dogs, try chewing on it. Dogs are "mouthy" — one of their ways of learning about the world is by their sense of taste and chewing. They are not being mischievous when they chew on things in your house; they are exploring with their teeth.

The downside to your puppy "exploring" with his teeth is that he considers anything in your house part of his lessons. So, when you bring a puppy into your home, you do need to make some adjustments, at least for the first few months. Put up anything you cherish to keep it away from your puppy's teeth. That includes remote controls, eyeglasses, shoes, purses, jewelry, and anything else your puppy can fit in his mouth.

You cannot hide everything from your puppy. If your puppy is chewing on furniture or woodwork, for instance, you can buy products like bitter apple to spray or apply. These products taste awful and should discourage your puppy from tasting things that smell like them.

Supervise puppies as much as possible until they prove they can be trusted in your home. If you bring a puppy into your house and give him the run of the place from day one, you basically are turning a little hellion loose in your house. Your puppy needs to learn some house manners, including the rules about chewing, before he earns the privilege of being free all over the house, especially when you are not watching him. Many people restrict a puppy to just a couple of rooms where he is allowed to play until he has proven that he can be trusted.

If you leave a puppy loose in your house when you are away from home, you are asking for trouble. Either confine your puppy to a couple of rooms where he cannot get into trouble or think about using a crate for your puppy while you are away from home for a few hours.

You can help your puppy tremendously by providing him with safe things to chew on. The more fun, interesting things your puppy has to chew on of his own, the less he will be tempted to chew on your things.

Keep in mind that all puppies will be losing baby teeth between the ages of 4 and 7 months and getting their adult teeth. During this time, they will have an irresistible urge to mouth and chew things. Make sure you provide them with all kinds of things to put in their mouths, from soft squishy things to hard chews.

Jumping up on people

One of the most common behavior problems with dogs, especially puppies and young adults, is jumping up on people. Dogs do this because they are unbelievably excited. They are happy. They want to show you how happy and

excited they are. They want to show you how much they really *really* like you.

Unfortunately, most people do not want dogs to show them how much they like them by jumping up on them. A dog jumping up on you can get muddy paws on you; knock you down; knock things out of your arms; tear your clothes; and scratch you — and it is just annoying.

Dogs of all ages can exhibit this problem — puppies, adolescent dogs, and even older dogs can continue to jump up on people. The problem often starts when a dog is a cute puppy. No one corrects the puppy, and the behavior continues throughout the dog's life.

Luckily, there are some good ways to teach a dog not to jump up on people. None of these methods is hard to teach, but they do take some practice and commitment from a dog's owner. If you are inconsistent and you allow your dog to jump up sometimes and not at other times, your dog will continue to jump up on people.

Ignore your dog

One of the easiest ways to teach your dog not to jump up on people is to ignore him when he does it. Say that your dog jumps up on you when you walk in the house. If you completely ignore him — do not speak to him, do not touch him, do not acknowledge him in any way — and you do this every time you come in the door, then it will not be long before your dog stops jumping up on you, especially if you only give your dog lots of petting and attention when he is standing calmly on the floor. The catch with this method is that it only works if every single person in the house does it. If even one person pets or speaks to your dog when he jumps up, then the whole lesson is ruined. Your dog will keep jumping up on people because he is getting attention for doing it. If you are out in public with your puppy you should tell strangers not to pet your puppy if he jumps up on them so he will not get any positive reinforcement from them.

Grab your dog's paws

This method will work for big dogs, but it does not work well for small dogs. When your big dog jumps up on you, grab their front paws (which might be on your chest or shoulders). Hold on to their paws for as long as you can, long after your dog wants to get down. The goal with this lesson is to make  jumping up on you not so much fun for your big dog. Because your big dog has to stand on his hind legs when he jumps up, he can only hold this position for a limited amount of time. When you keep him in this position longer than is comfortable for him, you are controlling the contact. This often discourages big dogs from jumping up.

You can see why this method does not work with small dogs. If you have to bend down to hold their paws, it defeats the purpose. Not only is bending down uncomfortable for you, but being face to face with a small dog gives him the positive reinforcement he wants.

Control the leash

Some people like to use a leash to teach their dog not to jump up on them. With your dog wearing a collar and leash, when your dog starts to jump up on you or someone else, step on the leash to bring your dog back to the standing position. This often works to keep the dog from jumping, but you have to be good at timing when to step on the leash. You also have to be pretty good at stepping precisely on the leash. Otherwise, if you miss stepping on the leash, your dog will jump up on someone.

Teach your dog good manners

You also can teach your dog some good manners when you or someone else comes in your door by teaching your dog to sit at the door instead of jumping up on people. Your dog should already know the "sit" command for this lesson. Make sure you have plenty of treats with you. You can have a friend or family member help you. Have them ring the doorbell or knock on the door. When your dog starts to get excited, give the "sit" command. He might not obey. If he does sit, praise him and give him lots of treats. If he jumps on the person, bring him back and try again. Do not punish. Keep trying with the sit command in this situation until he obeys. He should get bored with the same person coming through the door eventually, especially with that person not petting or speaking to him. Once he is sitting when your friend comes through the door, repeat to make sure he gets the lesson. You can repeat this lesson each day until he is solid with it. Always praise and reward your dog for showing his good manners and sitting when people come through the door. If you would like to really test your dog, you can take him to a friend's house and try the lesson there. Try him in other places.

These are some ways to teach your dog to stop jumping on people. You could try other variations, especially if your dog jumps on people outside the home or when greeting them on walks. You might need to use the leash method or the method of teaching your dog to sit when greeting people. Try different methods and see what works for your dog.

Behavior Problems of Adult Dogs

Miscommunication with your dog can occur when signals are crossed. You and your dog do not understand each other's communication. One of you is not communicating well or one of you is not understanding well, or both. Of course, because we are the humans, we usually put the blame on the dog, but it is not always the dog's fault. You might be the one with the behavior problem, but your dog is not able to tell you.

Miscommunication with a dog can take many forms, and it happens all the time. One of the most common is when a dog has an accident or soils in the house. This incident can happen for many reasons, but it often makes the dog's human angry when it does happen. Sometimes humans think dogs are willfully using the bathroom in the house or that the dog is taking revenge on them for something. The dog hates them, or the dog is "untrainable." All of these assumptions are unlikely. When a dog soils in the house, it usually has a simple explanation. The dog could not wait any longer to go outside, for example. Or, the dog was overfed and had an upset stomach. The dog might be ill and has diarrhea. There is often a physical or veterinary reason to explain why a dog might use the bathroom in the house. It is not a statement that the dog is trying to get even with the owner or acting out of spite, and it does not mean the dog is untrainable. In some cases, a dog has not been completely housetrained, and he might need more training. Unfortunately, this kind of miscommunication can have terrible consequences for a dog, and it is reported as one of the top reasons why owners take their dogs to shelters.

Misunderstandings Can Lead to Communication Problems

Miscommunication also can lead to some dog behavior problems. For example, some owners with toy dogs are inclined to treat them more like children than dogs. They do not like to correct them when they bark at people or challenge bigger dogs. They might let them start to become quite bossy in the home. In some cases, this can lead to toy dogs that might snap at people and behave badly. They can become tiny terrors in the home. Some people have labeled this behavior "small dog syndrome." It is entirely avoidable if the owner will treat the dog like a dog and not spoil them because they are so small and cute. But miscommunicating with the dog, giving him a false impression that he is in charge in the home, leads to serious behavior problems.

Something similar can occur in the case of dogs that are aggressive toward their owners. If the owner and dog have poor communication and the owner allows the dog to believe he is in charge in the home, the owner might find himself in fear of his dog. *Aggression will be discussed in more detail a little later in this chapter.*

Overcoming miscommunication and behavior problems like these are good reasons why it is important to improve your communication with your dog. Living with your dog involves communication and miscommunication. No one has perfect communication all the time, though you can work toward that goal.

In most cases, when you know why your dog is acting in a certain way, it can help you overcome undesirable behaviors. This is true in the case of behaviors like barking, digging, and separation anxiety, as well as some cases of aggression. All of these behaviors are normal for dogs, at the right place and time. They become problem behaviors when your dog displays them inappropriately. Understanding what motivates your dog can help you control them.

Barking

Barking is a normal behavior for dogs. If you have more than one dog, chances are you have learned to tune out much of your dogs' barking during the day. You probably do not notice when your dogs bark while they are playing outside or when they bark at squirrels, though you quickly  notice if they bark in alarm. Their barking probably has become a background noise for you unless they are barking to indicate something important. However, your neighbors might be more likely to notice the barking.

Dogs bark for many different reasons. Barking is not as important to dogs as body language, but it is still an important means of communication. Even if your dog's barking gets on your nerves, you should not try to make your dog completely stop barking. His barking could alert you to an intruder or a fire, for example.

If your dog is engaging in excessive or nuisance barking and you wish to teach him to stop, there are several simple ways to break the habit. If you are home during the day or your dog is barking at night, you can try the following methods:

The Shake Can

One good way to stop your dog's barking is by using a shake can. A shake can is an aluminum can, such as a soft drink can, which is half-filled with pennies or pebbles. Tape over the top of the can with duct tape. Use the can as a loud rattle to startle your dog when he starts to bark, telling him, "No!" or "No bark!" You can also use a plastic bottle half-filled with pennies or pebbles and put the cap back on top. When your dog begins to bark, shake the can or bottle strongly and give him the command. As soon as he stops the barking to look at you, which he probably will do in surprise, you should praise him and give him a treat for *not* barking. The shake can lets you do two things: It startles the dog into momentarily stopping his barking, and it gives you a chance to praise and reward your dog for the desired behavior (not barking). Obviously, the shake can method works best if you are close to your dog when he barks.

Squirting Your Dog

You also can stop your dog's barking with a spray bottle of water or a small water pistol. Again, this method works best if you are close to your dog when he barks. However, you can place small spray bottles or squirt guns at various points around your home so they will be handy if your dog starts to bark in different rooms. The idea of squirting your dog with water is the same as using the shake can. When your dog is engaged in undesirable barking, you want to startle him, in this case with a squirt of water, into stopping. As soon as he stops the barking you should praise and reward him with a treat to let him know that not barking is good.

When using a spray bottle or squirt gun, do not soak your dog with water. You only need to startle him and get his attention.

Clicker Training

You can also use the clicker to train your dog not to bark. This takes a little patience on your part but it can be done. Have some small treats with you, and when your dog is barking at something non-stop, wait until he stops for a moment. Click and treat as soon as he is quiet. Praise him and let him know that being quiet is good. Repeat this every time your dog gets quiet for a second. If your dog is a determined barker, this can take some time, but you can train your dog using the "quiet" command with this method. Say, "quiet" when you click and treat.

These methods work well if you are home with your dog when he barks. However, many dogs bark when their owners are not home. If your dog is barking at your neighbors, you can make an effort to introduce your dog to them, teach your neighbors your dog's name, and encourage your neighbors to give him treats. Sometimes if your neighbors become friends with your dog, the dog will stop barking at them, ending the problem.

If your dog is barking at squirrels, cats, or other things you cannot control when you are not home, that problem is harder to handle. Some people opt for bark collars in that case. Bark collars include both electronic collars and citronella spray collars that spray a citrus-like scent toward your dog's face to discourage him from barking. Regarding electronic collars, most dogs only have to try them once or twice, and then they respect them while the collars are on, so the dogs are not repeatedly shocked. However, if you remove the collar, the dog will resume his barking. Electronic collars are usually said to have the same effect as touching a doorknob after walking across carpet and getting a static charge. If you have questions about how they feel, you can try one on your own arm. They are unpleasant but not painful. Electronic dog collars can be triggered by the sound of barking or by vibrations from your dog's throat. Collars that are triggered by barking can be accidentally set off if another dog in the home barks and unfairly punish a dog. Collars that rely on throat vibrations only react when the dog wearing the collar barks. They generally are considered a better choice.

Digging

Digging is another normal dog behavior that is often not appreciated by humans. If you have one of the terrier breeds or a dachshund, this behavior is more likely to become a problem than  with most other breeds. These breeds were bred to dig and go into holes after vermin, foxes, and badgers. Many of these dogs will happily fill your yard with holes, especially if they scent a mole or some other prey underground.

Other dogs like to dig to make dens for themselves. You might see your dog digging out a nice cool spot under a bush to lie in on a hot day. Other dogs like to bury their toys or bones so they can come back for them later. And some dogs cannot seem to resist trying to dig out under fences.

There are different ways to handle digging problems, depending on the kind of digging your dog is doing. If your dog is digging holes in your yard to bury toys or bones, or just because he thinks it is fun to dig, you can discourage the digging by filling them in with pebbles or marble chips. Dogs will not dig on the pebbles or marble chips. You also could fill them in with dirt and cover them over with chicken wire. Chicken wire is practically invisible, grass will grow back, and your neighbors will never see the wire. Dogs do not like the feel of the wire on their paws so they will leave it alone. However, this will not stop your dog from digging new holes.

If your dog is determined to dig holes in your yard, you can set up a manual sprinkler. A manual system will allow you to turn the sprinklers on your dog when you catch him digging. Of course, some dogs might enjoy getting wet, but the sprinklers will startle most dogs into stopping their digging, especially if you combine the sprinklers with a firm, "No!" command.

If you have a garden and your dog is digging in it, you can try putting mothballs among your flowers. They will keep some dogs away. You also can buy products from your garden supply store to sprinkle in your garden to discourage dogs from bothering your flowers. However, if you have a vegetable or herb garden, there is probably nothing that will keep your dog from bothering your garden. You will need to fence off your garden or plant it where your dog cannot reach it. Dogs love vegetables and many herbs, and they will eat them if they have the chance.

If your dog is trying to dig under your fence, you can do several things to discourage him. The simplest thing is probably to purchase some attractive railroad timbers and line them along the base of your fence. Railroad timbers are heavy, and most dogs cannot move them; they will block most dogs from digging. You can also consider burying your fence deeper or placing chicken wire along the base of the fence. If you have a few soft spots where your dog keeps trying to dig out, try using some marble chips in these places. Your dog will not want to dig on these hard pieces of rock, and they will close up the soft holes.

You can provide your dog with his own digging spot in the yard by making him a sandbox. Buy some railroad timbers (or other sections of wood) and put them together to make a large box. Fill it with sand for your dog. Use play sand as you would for children. Then half-bury some of your dog's favorite toys and bones in the box. Call him over and start digging to show him that it is his space. Help him find his toys. Your dog should love the sandbox. You also can use a hard plastic kiddie pool as a sandbox.

Separation Anxiety

Lots of dog owners today have heard the term "separation anxiety." They might even think that their dogs have this problem. However, there is a difference between genuine separation anxiety and dogs that are sad when their owners leave them alone. Dogs are experts at playing on our emotions. When you go to work in the morning and your dog looks at you with big, pleading eyes, making you feel guilty for leaving him, it is normal for you to feel terrible. But rest assured that most dogs settle down and sleep while you are at work. They play, chew on chew toys, and find other ways to amuse themselves during the day. They are not experiencing separation anxiety, no matter how sad they look when you leave them, even if they bark or whimper for a few minutes.

On the other hand, a small number of dogs do not adjust to being left alone by their owners. It is hard to say whether they are worried more about being alone or about what will happen to you when you are away from them. Some dogs might feel an overprotective need to take care of you, and when you are out of their sight, they work themselves into a frenzy. Or it is possible that these dogs have abandonment issues, to put things in human terms. Many dogs with separation anxiety come from animal shelters, and they have been passed from person to person at an early age.

Whatever the case, if you have a dog that suffers from separation anxiety, it is not an easy problem to deal with. You usually can identify separation anxiety by the following behavioral signs:

- Barking or howling when the owner leaves
- Urinating or defecating in the house even when the dog is completely housetrained
- Chewing and digging on furniture in the home
- Destroying personal objects that have the owner's scent
- Pacing in the house
- Trying to escape

As you can see, these symptoms go far beyond the feelings shown by a dog that is saddened temporarily when his owner leaves the house.

Separation anxiety is a full-blown condition in dogs, and treatment often requires both medication and behavioral modification. The medication is given on a short-term basis and is used to interrupt the dog's feelings of anxiety so he can learn new, more positive behaviors with training. Medication alone does not usually solve the problem. Training by itself, by means of desensitization, usually only works in milder cases, as dogs are often too anxious to relax and focus on learning new behaviors.

If your dog has a serious case of separation anxiety, start by talking to your veterinarian and having your dog examined. Your vet can rule out any physical problems that could be causing your dog to have behavior problems such as hormonal changes or thyroid problems. You also will need to work with your vet if your dog needs any kind of medication. Your vet might be able to recommend a good dog trainer or animal behaviorist who specializes in working with dogs with separation anxiety.

If your dog has a milder problem with separation anxiety, it is still a good idea to see your vet so you can rule out any physical problems, but medication might not be necessary. You might be able to use desensitization techniques, explained in the next section, to teach your dog to overcome his separation anxiety.

Author Experiences: Jasper

Jasper might have loved me more than any dog I have ever had. He was a beautiful English setter, but he had been born deaf in one ear, so his breeder placed him in a pet home instead of keeping him to show. (Deaf dogs are not allowed to be shown at dog shows and should not be used for breeding.) She thought all was well until one day about a year later, unbelievably, a skinny Jasper appeared at the pound where she worked as a volunteer. It turned out that his family worked 14 hours a day and had no time for him. They had been leaving him in the backyard all day where he had gotten in trouble for barking, probably out of loneliness. Finally, they had just dumped him at the night drop for the pound instead of contacting Jasper's breeder, as their contract called for them to do if they could not keep him. His breeder took him home and got him back in shape, and then she put a notice in our breed club magazine to see if someone would like to take him as a pet. As soon as I read the ad, I thought I should call her. Next thing I knew, Jasper was getting off a plane, and I was going to him. It was love at first sight for both of us.

After all he had been through, Jasper had some problems he needed to overcome. He had a bad case of separation anxiety. He did not want me to be out of his sight even for a moment. He wanted to be touching my foot or leg all the time for comfort. He was also jealous if another dog took too much of my attention. I had to learn to read his body language so I could tell if he was comfortable or becoming anxious. I had to look for signs that he was becoming upset if I was petting another dog. I learned to read his eyes and watch his tail. I noticed his posture. He loved female dogs but hated puppies. He did not like old dogs. He could be unpredictable sometimes, but I was always looking for communication signals.

After about a year, I thought he had vastly improved. I was planning to take a trip to Florida to show my girl Sami at some shows. Jasper loved Sami, and I thought it would be nice to take him with me. Plus, I would not have to leave him behind with my mother where he might be anxious about me. The trip was going well until the day I brought Jasper to the show and crated him in the grooming tent. Friendly exhibitors and other friendly dogs surrounded him. I would only be gone for a few minutes while I showed Sami in the show ring. While I was showing her I became aware of some kind of commotion outside the ring, but I didn't know what it was. When we came out of the ring, there was Jasper with someone holding his collar. He had tried to run into the ring where Sami and I had been. Apparently, he had broken his way out of our crate and come racing across the outdoor show grounds to find us. That is separation anxiety. Over the years, he became much better, but I never tried taking him on a trip again. I think Jasper communicated to me, effectively, that he did not intend to allow me out of his sight.

Desensitization

Separation anxiety often manifests when the dog's owner has to leave the house, so one way to work on your dog's issue is by using desensitization techniques to help him get used to seeing you leave. The idea behind desensitization is to do something until it is no big deal, to put it simply. You practice doing all the things involved in leaving the house until your dog no longer gets anxious about seeing you leave, up to and including actually leaving. It can take weeks or even months to build up to leaving the house and being gone for short periods, but this is a good way to help a dog with separation anxiety overcome the problem.

For example, you could begin by picking up your keys and shaking them. This could make some dogs anxious. Let your dog get used to you doing this and seeing that nothing happens. Once your dog has accepted the keys, another day you can add your purse, briefcase, or something you take with you to work. Keep picking this object up until your dog learns to relax and accept that nothing bad happens. Gradually do things you do to prepare to go to work such as getting dressed and following your morning routine until your dog is no longer nervous about these things. Eventually, you can start going to the door. It might take some extra time for your dog to relax when he sees you at the door, but keep working on it. Go to the door but do not leave. Show your dog that nothing bad happens. Then you can work toward going outside the door and stepping back in the house. After that, work on staying outside for a couple of minutes. Then add going to your vehicle, and starting the vehicle. Work toward driving away for five minutes and returning.

During all of these milestones, if your dog becomes upset, you might have to go back to an earlier step where your dog was comfortable and slowly start to move forward again. If you are patient, your dog will continue to make progress.

You eventually should reach the point where you can drive away and stay away from the house for 45 minutes. Once you reach this amount of time, you should be able to leave your dog at home. Most dogs that experience separation anxiety will do so within the first 45 minutes that the owner is gone.

This technique will work for dogs with milder cases of separation anxiety, but you must be patient with your dog. Remember that he is trying to overcome a great deal of anxiety and fear when he sees you doing things that suggest you are going to leave him.

You can offer your dog treats and rewards while you are working on desensitization, but many dogs are not interested in food rewards when they are coping with anxiety and fear. Praise and petting often work better.

If desensitization does not work for your dog, talk to your vet about finding a good dog trainer or animal behaviorist who works with dogs with separation anxiety.

Separation anxiety tips

If you live with a dog that has separation anxiety, there are a few tips that might help you in dealing with your dog.

Crating your dog is often not a good idea. Your dog might try to bust out of the crate if he becomes frantic. He could injure himself or break his teeth trying to open the door.

Keep your emotions low-key. If you are overly sad or upset when you leave your dog, for example, your dog will believe there is something to be upset about. Stay calm and quiet when you arrive home and when you leave. Try to set a good example for your dog.

Obedience training for your dog helps. Training and good socialization help build your dog's confidence. Doing things that build your dog's confidence will help him be more independent instead of depending too much on you.

Socialize your dog when he is a puppy. Puppies that are well socialized are less likely to have problems with separation anxiety because they develop positive self-esteem and self-confidence.

It is never too late to socialize a dog. Even if you get an adult dog from a shelter and he has separation anxiety, you can work on his socialization. It will help all his issues, including the separation anxiety.

Encourage your dog to do "dog" things. Let him be a dog and have dog friends. The human-dog bond is important, but it is not good for your dog to rely exclusively on you for all his emotional needs. Allow him to have dog buddies and have interests beyond you, even if it is just watching squirrels.

Aggression

Aggression generally falls into two categories: aggression toward other dogs and aggression toward people. It is not unusual for dogs to feel or display aggression, but when dogs live in the home with us, such displays are usually unwanted and out of place. Any dog, under the right circumstances, can display some degree of aggression, whether it is the biggest, strongest dog, or a tiny toy dog. It is not breed specific. If you live with a dog, then sooner or later you are likely to have some head-to-head problem with your dog, even it if is only a minor skirmish over a toy or disagreement about getting a bath. A puppy might growl at you, or a 15-month-old male dog may feel rebellious and try to bite you when you insist on putting him in the bathtub, for example. Or a toy dog might snap at you when you try to make him move off the sofa. According to the Centers for Disease Control, about 800,000 people seek treatment for dog bites each year, and about half of those people go to an emergency room. Sixteen people die annually from dog attacks. Many of these bites happen to the dog's owner. Most of these bites are one-time problems that will never happen again because the dog learns he is not allowed to bite. Other bites happen to people who work in animal professions such as dog groomers, vets, and people in animal shelters, as you might expect. These professions encounter unruly dogs on a daily basis.

If your dog is threatening you and you fear he might bite you, contact a professional to help you. Dog aggression is a serious issue, and you might need to work with a professional dog trainer or animal behaviorist to help your dog.

Aggression toward other dogs

Dogs can display aggression toward other dogs for lots of reasons. If you have more than one dog in the home, the dogs could be fighting about status. There could be jealousy over toys, food, or territory such as a favorite sleeping spot, or  even jealousy over you. If you have an unaltered female dog in the home, two males could be fighting over her. Female dogs sometimes fight with each other, too. Dogs can fight about a lot of things.

The easiest way to deal with this kind of aggression in the home is to remove the thing that the dogs are fighting over, if possible. If you have two dogs fighting over a toy, remove the toy. Of course, it is not always possible to remove what the dogs are fighting about. If the dogs are fighting over your attention, you will need to make sure both dogs are getting their share of attention. If dogs are fighting over food, feed the dogs separately. You can feed them in different rooms or feed them in crates so each dog can eat his own food in peace.

In most cases, dogs will sort out their own status issues and figure out who is in charge among the dogs, but you should always be in charge in the house. The dogs should not have any doubt about your position. If you have an old dog and one of the other dogs is picking on him, you might need to step in and protect him. If you have a puppy that is pestering the adults, you might have to make the puppy behave. Dog aggression toward other dogs in the home is usually self-limiting, but when it is not, you need to be prepared to step in and stop any dogs that are being too aggressive toward other dogs.

If your dogs get into a knock-down-drag-out fight in the home, you have to deal with it as best you can. A pot of cold water thrown on the participants often will stop a fight, or you can use the water sprayer, if you have one, from your kitchen sink to spray the dogs with cold water. You also can throw a big blanket over both dogs, effectively stopping them from seeing what they are doing. This often will stop a fight while you drag each dog to a neutral corner or to separate rooms that you can shut off. They can cool down for a while until you are ready to let them out again. If you have a friend or family member with you, each of you can drag the back legs of one of the dogs and pull them off each other, and then deposit them in separate rooms. A dog focused on his adversary will rarely pay attention to someone pulling him away. He will remain focused on the dog in front of him.

If you have two dogs fighting in your backyard, turn your hose on them.

Fortunately, this kind of fight is extremely rare for most dog owners. If you do have two dogs get into this kind of fight, you can expect some hard feelings to linger. Do not be surprised if the dogs end up fighting again sometime soon, so be prepared. If you have two dogs that really start to hate each other, you could be forced to find a new home for one of the dogs in order to avoid scenes like this being repeated. Otherwise, the fighting probably will continue until one dog is beaten down and no longer acts like his normal self. He might be happier living in a home where he can be the only dog.

You also can encounter aggression toward your dog from another dog when you are out in public. This can be a hard situation to defuse. When you are out with your dog, taking a walk for example, pay attention to the body language of the dogs you encounter. Are the dogs relaxed and wagging their tails? Are they bouncing and playful? Are they minding their own business or paying attention to their owners? Or, does that dog have his eyes fixed on your dog in a challenging stare? Your dog probably is reading the body language of the dogs he sees, and you should be watching them, too. If you meet an aggressive dog, you will need to know what to do.

Many dog owners take an umbrella and/or pepper spray with them when they take their dogs for a walk, in the event that they meet an unpleasant dog. They can use the umbrella to hit the dog and try to keep him away or spray the dog with the pepper spray if he attacks. If you do not have these items, or you prefer not to use them, allow your dog to protect himself if he is attacked. Of course, if you have a small dog, pick him up and leave immediately! But if you have a larger dog and you cannot pick him up if another dog lunges toward him, you should let go of the leash and allow your dog to defend himself. If you hold onto the leash, you could cause your dog to be injured. You could even end up in the middle of the fight yourself. So, if another dog attacks when you are walking your dog, drop the leash, and get out of the way. Once the dogs are engaged with each other, you (and perhaps the other owner) can try to separate the dogs by dragging them away from each other by their rear legs. Once the dogs are separated, you can assess injuries and, if no one is seriously injured, go home.

Whatever you do, when dogs are fighting, do not try to step between them. That is a sure way to get bitten. Your dog does not have his mind on you at that moment, and he is not looking where he is putting his teeth. You could be seriously injured if you come near a dog's head at this time.

Aggression toward people

Dogs are not born bad, mean, or aggressive. They are social animals, and they are happy to live in a pack structure. They come into our homes and willingly accept humans as their leaders. Aggression usually develops when there is miscommunication or a misunderstanding about the dog's role in the home, and the dog begins to think he should be in charge.

Growling

It is not uncommon for puppies to growl at people. If your puppy growls at you, it does not mean that your puppy is going to grow up to become an aggressive dog or that he is a "bad" dog. It means that he is displaying an ordinary dog behavior. Puppies growl at their brothers and sisters. Sometimes they cross the boundary and growl at people, too. However, it is inappropriate for him to growl at you, and the sooner he learns this fact, the better. The best thing to do if a small puppy growls at you is to ignore him completely. Do not respond to him at all. If you pet him or encourage him, he will think that growling is a good behavior. If you punish him, he is getting negative attention, but it is still attention, and he will just have more to complain about. If he growls at you when you are trimming his nails or making him do something he does not want to do, ignore it, and continue doing what you are doing. Puppies are bluffing to see what you will do. Ignore the behavior and show your puppy that his growling is meaningless.

The exception is when a puppy growls at a child. Puppies and dogs often see children as equals because of their small size and lack of power in the home. They recognize that children are not in charge, so they feel freer to challenge them. Do not allow puppies and children to play together without supervision. If a puppy growls at a child, end the play right away. Put the puppy in a time-out.

When a puppy learns early on that growling is inappropriate, there are usually no more problems later. He will be satisfied with his role in your home.

If an adult dog growls at you in your home, take it more seriously. An adult dog that growls at you could bite you. A growl is a warning in this case, as is snapping or a dog that bares his teeth. In these cases, you might need to consult a professional such as a dog trainer who specializes in dealing with aggressive dogs or an animal behaviorist. If you ever feel fearful of your own dog, talk to a professional.

Guarding behavior

One of the ways that aggression often manifests in the home is when dogs display guarding behavior. Examples of this kind of behavior include dogs that guard a beloved toy and refuse to give it up or dogs that guard their food and growl or bite at anyone who attempts to pick up the bowl. In situations like these, the dog might end up biting his owner.

There are ways to overcome guarding behavior. Of course, it is best if you can prevent these behaviors from starting when your dog is a puppy, but even if your dog is already displaying these problems, you can try the following solutions.

Teaching your dog to swap: If your dog tends to guard toys or other objects and refuses to give them up, try teaching him to swap or trade with you. Get some of your dog's favorite treats.

They must be something that he loves. When he has the toy or object that he guards, offer him the treat in exchange for the object. If he accepts the trade, be generous and give him lots of his favorite treat to make it worth his while. Give your dog another toy and then offer to trade him for it with his favorite toy. Always make the trades beneficial to him so he trusts you to give him something good. Do not try to keep his favorite toy away from him, but teach him that it is OK to give it up because he will get something better. If you practice swapping with your dog, he will stop guarding the object so much and stop displaying the aggressive behavior over it.

Giving food: If your dog guards food, particularly refusing to allow you to take a bowl from him, you can do a couple of different things to remind him not to bite the hand that feeds him.

Because your dog seems to be afraid you are going to take his food away, you can prove to him that the opposite it true. When your dog is next to his food bowl, casually drop in some tasty things to eat at every meal. Toss a piece of baked chicken in the bowl or a few bites of steak, for example. Make sure your dog sees you dropping these delicious bites into his bowl. Let your dog begin to look for the good things you add to his ordinary kibble. Instead of guarding his bowl, he should begin to wait and hope you will give him something good. Adding these tasty bites to your dog's bowl should remind him that all good things come from you, and he should begin to stop guarding the bowl as much.

If your dog is still having a problem with guarding his food, you can try completely removing the bowl. This is a drastic step, but you can begin feeding your dog by hand, one piece of kibble at a time. This is a definite way to remind your dog of where his food comes from. Your dog will have to earn his bowl again by showing good manners about his food. When your dog is hungry, he will take the food from your hand and do it without growling. It usually only takes a short time before the dog is willing to display better manners at meal time.

Other kinds of aggression in the home

Other kinds of aggression in the home can be more difficult to overcome and usually need to be treated on an individual basis. If your dog becomes aggressive when you try to make him move from a favorite spot,  for example, this kind of confrontation can escalate into the owner getting bitten. From the owner's perspective, this is an innocent misunderstanding. You could invite your dog to get on the sofa, perhaps, because you love him and want to pet him. Your dog is happy to get on the sofa because this is an indication of his high status in the home, and it is comfortable. As time goes by, the dog feels that it is his right to occupy the sofa, and he is the top dog in the home. One day when you tell the dog to get down because you want to sit there, the dog is outraged because he thinks you are challenging his position. The situation can end up with you being bitten. This is a classic case of miscommunication about what being on the sofa means to the dog and owner.

There is nothing wrong with allowing your dog to get on furniture. Most Americans probably do allow their dogs to get on furniture. But when you allow your dog to have privileges such as this, it is important to remind him that you are still in charge in the home. Otherwise, your dog can react with aggression when you do something to challenge what he considers as his position in the home.

If your dog is displaying forms of aggression in the home, one of the best things you can do is begin obedience training. Training your dog, even to obey basic commands, begins to put you back in charge. You might need to work with a professional on specific problems in the home, but obedience training, especially with a good instructor, can start helping your overall relationship with your dog and restore your position as the one in charge. If your dog already has been trained and he is being aggressive in the home, you will need to go over his training again as a refresher course to remind him you are in charge.

Regarding the situation with the sofa, if your dog growls at you when you tell him to move, do not force the issue and get bitten. Instead, start training your dog and working on his manners or retraining your dog. If you have previously trained your dog at home, look for a training class and work with a trainer. You also should remove the "perks" your dog enjoys in the home.

We love our dogs and give them lots of freedom to share our homes, but that freedom is contingent on good behavior. If your dog is challenging you and behaving aggressively, take away your dog's privileges until he earns them again with good behavior. Require your dog to sit politely before you feed him. Require him to sit politely and wait for you to open the door for him to go outside. Restrict him to sleeping in his crate at night and not on your bed. Sleeping on your bed is a tremendous privilege for a dog that gives him status that is nearly equal to your own. If your dog is behaving badly, remove this privilege until his behavior improves. And, finally, you should require your dog to sit politely and wait to be invited to sit beside you on the sofa, if you decide to allow him to get up there.

Another situation where a professional trainer or animal behaviorist might be needed is if your dog becomes possessive or jealous over a family member. It is not unusual for a dog to have a special bond with one member of the family, whether it is an adult or child. But if your dog threatens other family members over trivial things or tries to guard one member of the family from other people in the family, this can be a dangerous situation, and you should seek out a professional. (Obviously, this does not include home situations where there is physical abuse and a dog protecting someone. In those cases, the dog is acting appropriately.)

Most dogs rarely display any kind of aggression in the home or toward people. These suggestions should help when dogs guard food or objects or display minor problems. Remember: if you ever feel threatened by your dog, contact a professional dog trainer or animal behaviorist for help.

CHAPTER EIGHT

Advanced Communication

If you have spent time socializing your dog and working with him on basic obedience lessons, you could be wondering, what now? You probably have a happy, well-behaved dog,  and the two of you enjoy good communication with each other. So, what else is there for you to do together?

There is an entire world of dog sports, activities, and events open to well-trained, well-socialized dogs. There are even serious jobs for such dogs if you would like to contribute to your community. Purebreds, mixed breeds, and dogs of all sizes can take part in these activities. As an owner, you do not need to have any special qualifications to participate in most of these events and sports, unless it is something you and your dog have to qualify for together, such as passing a test for therapy dog work.

One of the best ways to strengthen the bond between you and your dog is do things together that you both enjoy. You might find that some of the events and kinds of canine work discussed here would be of interest to you and your dog, so consider trying them.

Dog Sports and Fun Activities

There are many different kinds of dog sports and fun activities for dogs and their owners in North America today. Some of them are based on things dogs do by instinct such as herding tests for herding dogs, or field events for bird dogs; and some events are things all dogs can enjoy such as running timed obstacle courses in agility or catching Frisbees. Just like people, different dogs like different things and are good at different sports.

Most of the dog sports and fun activities discussed in this section are held through the auspices of various kennel clubs or organizations that supervise these events. Sometimes, a local training club owns equipment, so members can meet to practice. Or, people can practice at home with their dogs. Some events do not require much equipment, while others do. If you are interested in getting involved, find out if there is a local club in your area. Other dog owners involved with the sport can be helpful as you get started. You also can visit the national club online for more information about the exact rules of the sport. If there is more than one national club for a sport, as in the case of agility, the rules can be slightly different for each organization, so check them out carefully. The national clubs that offer events are indicated in each section.

AKC's Canine Good Citizen® (CGC) training

The American Kennel Club's Canine Good Citizen program is open to all dogs, purebred and mixed breed. Any dog can train for this test and earn this title. The CGC title is awarded to dogs that show they are "good citizens." This means they have good manners and know how to behave well around people and other dogs in public. Many state legislatures have designated passing the Canine Good Citizen program as proof that a dog is well behaved. Some insurance companies accept the CGC title as proof that your dog is well trained and well behaved. Insurance companies can charge higher premiums for certain breeds, but a CGC title can offset these costs. And passing the Canine Good Citizen test often can be accepted by therapy dog organizations to meet their qualifications. Dogs who pass their CGC test are ready to move on to obedience training, rally, agility, or any other dog activities because they have a good foundation. This program already is making a positive impact on many communities by encouraging responsible dog ownership.

The Canine Good Citizen program began in 1989 as a way to reward dogs that have good manners at home and in the community. The program is aimed at both the owner and the dog; it emphasizes responsible dog ownership and good behavior for the dog. There are ten steps in the CGC test, and a dog that passes the test receives a certificate from the AKC. He also can add the CGC title to his name.

Canine Good Citizen training is basic training for a dog. Dogs that are well socialized, friendly, and comfortable having strange people and unknown dogs around them will do well on the test. The purpose of the training is to help your dog get used to the kind of situations that will happen during the test, such as being petted by a friendly stranger, having unexpected noise happening near him, and so on. Your dog does not have to know a lot of obedience, though knowing some basic obedience is always helpful.

As a result of completing the CGC training, your dog becomes better socialized and more comfortable when he is out in public meeting people and encountering other dogs. And you have a dog that is a pleasure to own, that is always welcome wherever he goes because he knows how to behave.

In order to pass the AKC's Canine Good Citizen Test, your dog needs to accept a friendly stranger, sit politely for petting, allow someone to groom him with a brush or comb and pick up his paws, walk on a loose leash, walk through a crowd, sit and lie down on command, and stay while the owner walks 20 feet away. The dog has to come when called from 10 feet away.

The dog has to behave politely around other dogs and show no more than casual interest when another dog stops a few feet away. The dog has to stay calm and confident when faced with a distraction such as a jogger running by or someone dropping a chair. And, with the dog on his leash, the owner has to go out of sight for three minutes. The dog should stay calm while the owner is absent and not become upset.

So, you can see that the test can be challenging, but with some training and practice, your dog can earn his title. The AKC offers the test through various local kennel clubs. Certified evaluators evaluate your dog. Kennel clubs, dog training clubs, and animal shelters offer classes to help people and their dogs prepare for the test. Evaluators can teach classes leading up to the test, too. For more information about the Canine Good Citizen test you can visit the AKC website at **www.akc.org/events/cgc**.

Obedience Competitions

Many owners pursue obedience training at home with their dogs or take a few obedience classes because they want to have a well-trained dog. But kennel clubs also offer obedience trials

and tests as companion dog events. Dogs and their owners can train to become more proficient and earn increasingly advanced titles in obedience. Along with purebred dogs, both the American Kennel Club (AKC) and the United Kennel Club (UKC) allow mixed breed dogs to compete in obedience and other dog events, except conformation dog shows, if the dogs are registered in their mixed breed programs (Canine Partners and Limited Privilege, respectively). Mixed breed dogs must be spayed or neutered.

Dogs and their owners can compete at different levels, depending on their training level. Skills tested range from basics of sit, heel, and come to advanced levels that include directed retrieves over jumps and scent discrimination among different articles with the dog asked to choose the one that the handler has held and bring it back to the handler.

In an obedience trial, the dog begins with a perfect score of 200 points, and the judge deducts points as the dog and owner attempt to complete all required exercises. Your score is the number that remains when you finish. Passing scores are those of 170 and above. If you and your dog pass, you have earned a "leg" toward your title. For example, three passes, or "legs," are required to earn the AKC Companion Dog (CD) title, the novice obedience title. You must earn the novice title before you can move up to try to earn the Companion Dog Excellent (CDX) title in the open class, and you must earn the CDX title before you can move on to the next title, Utility Dog (UD), and so on. Each level becomes increasingly more demanding. Perfect scores of 200 are possible, but they are rare.

Along with individual obedience work, some people enjoy team obedience, working in groups of four handlers and four dogs to execute commands and perform training exercises with precision. You can form a team with friends or anyone you know who has dogs. All four dogs perform the commands at the same time.

If you are interested in training with your dog toward your CD title, focus on your dog's basic obedience commands and make sure he can execute them flawlessly and without hesitation. The setting at a dog show always provides some distractions, so make sure that your dog will obey you even when there are other things going on competing for his attention.

Depending on the show you are entering, visit the AKC site (**http://www.akc.org/dog_shows_trials/obedience**) or the UKC site (**www.ukcdogs.com/WebSite.nsf/WebPages/ DogObedience**), and familiarize yourself with the rules and the exercises you and your dog will be asked to perform.

Training at home is important, but it often helps to get in touch with your local kennel club or dog training club for additional support. Members of these clubs usually are experienced when it comes to participating in obedience and other dog events, and they can help you and your dog prepare. These clubs also might have some matches or tests set up before the event; so you and your dog can have a trial run.

Agility

Agility began as a sport in the UK a few years ago, but it has taken off and is growing fast in the U.S. and Canada today. The basic idea is simple. The dog races around an obstacle course as quickly as possible without knocking things down. Events are timed, and the dog with the best time wins. The owner is on the course with the dog but cannot touch him. The owner is allowed to coach and give the dog commands while he races around the course.

There are classes for all levels of dogs from those just beginning agility to the most advanced dogs. Courses become more difficult as the dog becomes more experienced. Courses are colorful and full of jumps, hoops, tunnels for the dogs to run through, A-frames, seesaws, and weave poles. At designated spots on the course, the owner might have to give the dog obedience commands such as a down-stay or a release. The dog does everything off leash.

Agility is exciting for dogs and handlers, and it is popular with spectators. Agility is even broadcast on television sometimes. Although it is fun, it is also a competition.

In North America, five main organizations hold agility events: the American Kennel Club (AKC), Canine Performance Events (CPE), United States Dog Agility Association (USDAA), the United Kennel Club (UKC), and North American Dog Agility Council (NADAC). The agility events sponsored by these organizations have many things in common. They are generally open to all dogs, even events held by the AKC and UKC, as long as you register your dog with their mixed breed program. Events are divided so that small dogs do not have to compete against large dogs. Jumps are kept to an appropriate size for small and large dogs, so a small dog does not have to jump something that is much too big for him. There are all kinds of events to make things more fun for owners and dogs, so not every course is the same.

There are also some differences between the groups. UKC is considered a good way to begin competing in agility because of their courses and the friendly atmosphere at their shows, but it is not easy to find UKC shows in every area. With other groups, some courses might be smaller and tighter while other courses could be bigger. Depending on your dog, you might prefer one kind of course to another. Jump heights can vary slightly between the groups, too. You can find out more about the different organizations and what their rules and requirements are by visiting them online for more information:

- 🐾 AKC agility: **http://www.akc.org/dog_shows_trials/agility**
- 🐾 Canine Performance Events: **www.k9cpe.com**
- 🐾 USDAA: **www.usdaa.com**
- 🐾 UKC agility: **www.ukcdogs.com/WebSite.nsf/Web Pages/DogAgility**
- 🐾 NADAC: **www.nadac.com**

If you are interested in getting involved in agility, you can train at home, but you will need some equipment to simulate the kind of obstacles your dog will encounter on the agility course. You can make some of these obstacles yourself, such as using a tire for a hoop your dog can jump through. You also can purchase agility starter sets from vendors. Starter sets usually come with three pieces of agility equipment such as a hurdle, a hoop, and some weave poles. You can add additional pieces, as you need them.

Many people prefer to train with a local kennel club or dog training club. The advantage of training at a club is that they often already have a complete set of agility obstacles. You also can gain valuable advice from talking to club members and having them critique your training. They often can offer tips to improve your dog's performance.

Rally

Rally is something of a cross between agility and obedience. Owners take their dogs through a course, on or off leash depending on the dog's level, performing different exercises. There are no interruptions from a judge giving directions. The directions for each exercise are printed on signs set throughout the course. It is perfectly all right to talk to your dog and encourage him all the way through the exercises. Rally was created with the ordinary dog owner in mind. Dogs and owners can move at their own pace, whether that is slow or fast. The emphasis is on having fun with your dog. However, rally is competitive; points are scored and standings are kept.

A rally course has ten to 20 stations depending on the level of difficulty. Exercises are not scored as precisely as they are for formal obedience competition. For instance, no one will demand that your dog heel perfectly at your side. However, there should always be a strong sense of teamwork between the owner and the dog.

Rally has varying levels of difficulty, and dogs and their handlers can progress through higher and higher levels by earning a title at each level. In AKC Rally, a dog can earn the Rally Novice title, the Rally Advanced title, and the Rally Excellent title.

Rally is usually considered to be the exciting form of obedience, so if you find doing obedience with your dog dull work, the two of you could enjoy rally. Sometimes, being able to talk to your dog and give him lots of positive encouragement during an exercise makes a big difference.

Flying disc

For dogs that love to catch Frisbees, there is the sport of flying disc, or disc dog. Disc dog is based on the action of

the owner throwing the disc for the dog and the dog making spectacular catches. Dogs have lots of fun chasing and catching the disc, and fans love to watch. Competitions are open to all dogs. The sport has competitive trials that test dogs for accuracy in catching the discs as well as for distance. Style also counts. Dogs and their owners can also compete on teams. Several organizations hold tournaments in the U.S. such as the UFO World Cup Final (**www.ufoworldcup.org**), the U.S. Disc Dog Nationals (**www.usddn.com**), and Skyhoundz® (**www.skyhoundz.com**).

Flyball

Flyball is another popular sport for dogs and their owners. Flyball pits relay teams of dogs racing against each other. The dog streaks down a short course over small hurdles toward a box, touches the box and makes a ball pop out, grabs the ball, and then races back toward his teammates so the next dog can set out on the course. Fastest team wins. The sport is fast, exciting, and lots of fun for all of the dogs and team members. In North America the North American Flyball Association (NAFA) (**www.flyball.org**) oversees the sport. Flyball teams are found virtually everywhere these days, and it is easy enough to start your own group with some friends.

Musical freestyle

Canine freestyle is what many of us call dog dancing. It is basically a choreographed performance of dog and owner with music. It is also known as heelwork to music, and this is how the training is often done for this sport. If you can teach your dog to heel and follow basic commands, then you can teach him the moves required to dance to music. Canine freestyle is often presented as a demonstration, but the World Canine Freestyle Organization (**www.worldcaninefreestyle.org**) also holds events for judging; so, dogs can receive titles. The Musical Dog Sports Association (**www.musicaldogsport.org**) holds workshops and demonstrations, as does the Canine Freestyle Federation (**www.canine-freestyle.org**). Canine freestyle can be a beautiful event to watch as the dog and human move together in choreographed steps to carefully chosen music.

Dock jumping (Air dog)

If you have seen Purina's Incredible Dog Challenge and watched dogs go airborne to splash down in the water, then you have seen dock jumping, or air dog. Labrador retrievers often excel at this sport, but you do not have to have a Lab to compete. Any dog that loves the water can enjoy it. The big-diving Labs on TV can sometimes make 20-foot jumps to retrieve a training dummy, but small dogs that love the water can make a splash, too.

Dock jumping events are offered by the United Kennel Club (**www.ukcdogs.com/WebSite.nsf/WebPages/DogDockJumping**), along with some other organizations that specialize in the sport such as Splash Dogs (**http://splashdogs.com**), Dock Dogs® (**www.dockdogs.com**), and Ultimate Air Dogs (**http://ultimateairdogs.com**).

As with many other canine activities and sports, you can train at home, but you will probably benefit from training with a club devoted to the sport. This is particularly true in the case of dock jumping, as it requires access to water. You will be able to work on your dog's retrieving at home, but at some point he will need to practice diving.

Schutzhund

In German, "Schutzhund" means "protection dog." Schutzhund training was developed to test German shepherds and ascertain if they were fit for protection work. These days, however, Schutzhund training is used as a way to evaluate any of the breeds that are used for the same kind of work.

Schutzhund training is made up of three parts. It consists of obedience, tracking skills, and the kind of protection work needed by police dogs. The training demonstrates a dog's usefulness and intelligence.

During the tracking portion of the test, the dog works with the handler on a 33-foot leash. An assistant lays down a trail for the dog some time before the test and drops small objects along the way. When the dog finds a scented object, he typically lies down with the object between his front paws to indicate he has found it. Dogs are evaluated on their accuracy and intensity as well as other factors.

In the obedience portion of the test, two dogs are in the field at the same time. One dog is put in a down-stay while the other dog works. The dog is given typical obedience commands, along with different retrieves and other commands. Gunshots also are fired to see how the dogs react to loud noises. The dogs must not be cringing or nervous. Dogs are evaluated on accuracy, eagerness, focus, and other factors that would be important in a police dog.

In the protection portion of the testing, there is a judge and an assistant. The assistant wears a padded sleeve and will perform various tasks on the course during the tests. There are also some "blinds" or places where the assistant can hide. The dog will be told to find the assistant. When he finds him, he will bark. At other times, the dog will be given commands to hold the assistant in place or to bite the sleeve. The dog must show that he has courage and that he is always under the control of the handler.

If you are considering Schutzhund work, it is important to have the right dog. A stable, reliable temperament in the dog is essential. The dog must be under control at all times. Dogs doing Schutzhund work do not act out of anger and or displaying aggression. They are performing a job as they have been trained to do, and they must stop when told.

Not every dog is a good candidate for Schutzhund training. Breeds that typically perform Schutzhund work well include the German shepherd, the Belgian Malinois, the Black Russian terrier, rottweilers, Dobermans, giant schnauzers, and some others. It would be unusual to find a sporting breed or a hound excelling at Schutzhund because they usually have different instincts. A clumber spaniel or a basset hound are unlikely to launch themselves in an attack on an intruder no matter how much you train them.

Schutzhund training can be challenging for a dog and an owner. It is often a good idea to work with an experienced instructor if you are new to Schutzhund. Most Schutzhund training in the United States is associated with the United Schutzhund Clubs of America (USA) (**www.germanshepherddog.com**) or with the German Shepherd Dog Club of American-Working Dog Association (**www.gsdca-wda.org**).

Herding, hunting, earthdog, weight pulling, tracking

The AKC and the UKC also offer many performance events. These include events such as field trials, hunting tests, herding trials, earthdog tests, weight pulls, and lure coursing.

There are even terrier races such as races for Jack Russell terriers. Some of these events are limited to particular breeds. The purpose of the test can be to verify that the breed still maintains the breed's original instincts for hunting or herding. Whatever the case, performance events usually require some larger area for hunting or other activities. They usually are not offered at a dog show venue, but you can find out information about them at a dog show or by visiting the AKC or UKC websites: **www.akc.org/dog_shows_trials/field_events** or **www.ukcdogs.com/WebSite.nsf/WebPages/DogWhat KindsOfShows**.

If you have a terrier or dachshund, or another breed that loves to "go to ground," then earthdog could be just what your dog will love. Earthdog trials are for breeds that were used at one time to hunt rats and other vermin. Dogs of these breeds love to dig and hunt creatures in the soil. These events use a narrow tunnel that is reinforced with wooden sides. There is an exit at each end so dogs cannot become lodged inside. The tunnels have been scented with a natural prey of the dogs, such as a rat. Then the dog is let loose inside the tunnel to find his prey. The prey is caged and cannot hurt the dog or be injured by the dog. The trial will test your dog's natural instincts, and your dog probably will have a great time doing what he was born to do. AKC offers titles for breeds that are approved to participate in earthdog events.

If you have a dog from a herding breed such as a border collie, sheltie, or Australian shepherd, you and your dog could enjoy herding tests. Many dogs from herding breeds have natural herding instincts. Your dog could try to herd you, your children, or your other pets at home, for example. If you have noticed that your dog has this instinct, consider giving him a chance to herd something else. A kennel club, a dog training club, or a breed club for your dog's breed could put you in touch with someone who trains dogs for herding. Herding tests basically test a dog's instincts and do not require the dog to have more advanced skills. You could attend a couple of training sessions and sign up for the test to see how your dog does. He will probably have a good time. He might be asked to herd some ducks or sheep while you guide him. Herding tests and more advanced trials are offered by the AKC, UKC, and some breed organizations to preserve herding instincts in herding breeds and to promote herding dogs as working dogs.

Despite urbanization, millions of people in the U.S. today continue to enjoy hunting with dogs. Hunting and fieldwork are things that dogs love, too, whether they are bird dogs like pointers, Irish setters, and Labrador retrievers; scent hounds such as beagles, foxhounds, and coonhounds; or sight hounds such as whippets, greyhounds, and salukis. People have been using salukis for more than 6,000 years and greyhounds for more than 4,000 years. Bloodhounds date back to the time of the Romans. Spaniels and setters date back to the 13th and 14th centuries. Many of the other hunting breeds were developed hundreds of years ago. The instinct to hunt with their human partners is deeply ingrained within these dogs. If you have a hunting breed, your dog would likely enjoy the opportunity to go out in the field at least a few times to exercise his instincts.

The AKC and the UKC both offer a wide range of hunting programs for dogs and their owners, ranging from hunting tests for pointing dogs and retrievers to events for flushing breeds such as spaniels to coon hunts. There are field trials for many different breeds, including dogs that hunt in packs such as beagles. Titles vary, depending on the breed and the events.

There are also specialist organizations for different hunting interests such as the Amateur Field Trial Clubs of America offering field trials for pointing breeds. It is not easy to become an AFT champion. The North American Versatile Hunting Dog Association (NAVHDA) (**www.navhda.org**) is dedicated to promoting versatile hunting dog breeds, i.e., dogs that can "dependably hunt and point game, retrieve on both land and water, and track wounded game on both land and water." Most of the breeds NAVHDA considers "versatile" are breeds from continental Europe that were developed in the 19th century such as the Weimaraner and vizsla, along with a few British breeds. As you might imagine, it can be quite difficult to earn titles from these specialist organizations.

As with other dog sports and activities, it helps to have a dog that is eager to learn and that has natural ability. If you and your dog would like to get involved in a hunting event, it is a good idea for you to attend an event first without your dog so you can see what the event is like, meet people, and find out what you might need in terms of equipment. Then you can start on some basic training. Like other sports, good basic obedience is important. You need to know that your dog will respond to you in the field even if he is on the scent of a bird or other prey. Once you have polished your basic obedience, talk to people involved with the sport to find out how to proceed. It is sometimes a good idea to work with a local trainer or hunter to "start" your dog on birds, for example. Sometimes there are bird dog training clubs in an area. It would be helpful to work with such a club.

You can order quail wings from hunting catalogs and use them for training or purchase them from hunters sometimes, but it is even better to work with live birds, such as quail, if you have the opportunity. You sometimes can buy them from people who raise them for several dollars each. If you have training grounds in your area, you can "plant" the birds by putting them under the cover of brush or bushes so your dog can practice finding them.

You do not need to worry about introducing your dog to a gun or any loud noises at this point. It is better if you do not. The AKC's Junior Hunter test for novice dogs does not use a gun for birds. You do not want your dog to become gun-shy this early in his training.

Many dogs love fieldwork and will try to drag you to the door so you can take them out. If your dog has the instinct to hunt, consider giving him a chance to show what he can do.

CASE STUDY: PAT AND HER SETTERS

Pat Boldt, AKC Breeder of
Merit of Irish Setters
Norco, California

I have had dogs for 44 years. I have ten living in my home and more co-owned living with families

Most of the time, I can tell what my dogs want when they look at me. In odd or non-routine situations or when they don't feel good, it's harder to tell. Again, most of the time I know what my dogs' barks mean. There is the "I'm hungry" bark, "I want to play now" bark, "look at me" bark, and the protective "someone's invading my territory" or "I'm protecting the yard" bark. Each dog has unique personality, so I don't try to understand other people's dogs' barks unless there is a reason to.

Here is a list of some of the everyday words my dogs know:

#1 Cookie!

#2 Kennel

#3 Dinner/breakfast

#4 Come

#5 Heel

#6 Sit

#7 Down

#8 Stand

#9 Do your business

#10 Good dog

#11 Bad dog

#12 no

#13 off

#14 gentle

#15 Toy

#16 Ball

#17 Find It

#18 Finish

#19 Front

#20 Wait

#21 Stay (I teach wait and stay to my dogs. Wait means you will sit or down here until I tell you to come to me. Stay means I'm leaving, and you will not move until I return!)

#22 Pee pee

#23 Table (grooming)

These are not in any particular order, other than cookie is by *far* the most recognized word. Because I have dogs ranging from puppies to veteran adults — my oldest right now is 10.5 years young — their vocabularies range by their training and maturity.

I train at home. I do obedience and AKC Rally events. Several of us try to meet to practice rally and obedience and help each other. I also belong to an all-breed obedience club that supports and encourages obedience training. It gets easier as you train more dogs and learn that you are frequently the problem. Example: Dogs cue off your body language; they are also masters of learning routine. The tone of your voice and your body language cue the dogs. Hand signals work in many situations better than verbal commands, and I am starting to use more hand signals than verbals. They begin to anticipate what you want because they want to please you … and to get the treat! All of my girls are food motivated, my boys not as much. They need more physical contact and verbal praise.

Maggie is training right now for her CD title having completed her Beginner Novice and Rally Novice obedience titles. So now, it is a big jump from mostly on leash to now mostly off-leash exercises. I have to "change up" the exercises so she does not anticipate because of routine what is being asked of her. Also, a good place for people to practice off-leash behavior in a different environment than their backyard is in an enclosed tennis court. That is where I first proof my dogs after working on off-leash activities before I go to a park or other area off leash.

If I want her to heel, I always start on my left foot. If I am leaving her for a wait or stay or walk around or any leaving action, I lead off on my right foot. It gets to a point where you don't really even need the verbal — they cue from your feet.

We filmed a commercial recently, and the agency asked if Maggie could do a recall. I said sure no problem. In Beginner Novice, the recall is about 20 feet. In CD, it's about 30 to 35 feet. Well, when you are on a beach about 100 to 125 feet away with waves crashing, your dog can't hear you. A hand signal finally worked each take!

Something I would do differently on the next litter is that I didn't teach "off," no jumping, at an early age and, in hindsight, allowed them to jump and petted them and talked to them as youngsters. It's better to teach the no jumping and have all four paws on the ground from the start!

With a pack, communication is much more complicated than with an individual dog. The dynamics are very, very different. Knowing who is the alpha male and the alpha bitch and maintaining balance with the youngsters as they begin to challenge the hierarchy can sometimes be difficult. Older, veteran age dogs and bitches no longer tend to want to be alpha, and the pack mentality can change quickly. I think consistency in training and understanding the pack is important. When I train a dog I usually, especially with puppies or youngsters, never go for more than ten-minute intervals. Older dogs can go longer as long as they are enjoying the training activity. I wish I didn't have to work and could just train the dogs all day! More time to train, that's my goal!

Keep it simple. Be consistent. Have fun. Not every dog, or owner for that matter, likes obedience. It's a very disciplined event. Maybe rally or agility is more fun. Build a foundation with basic behaviors and determine what each of your dogs want to do. I have two 18-month-old girls from my last litter. Both show in conformation. One loves to hunt. The other likes birds but hates burrs and weeds. She *loves* carrying toys in her mouth and doing basic obedience. The one completed a Junior Hunter title with little to no training. The other will likely do very well in rally and obedience.

Dogs like to have "jobs." They like having something to do that they are good at. It's your job to figure out what that is. Maybe it's guarding the backyard from squirrels and birds or supervising you while you garden. It might be as simple as letting them take all the toys out of the toy box and then teaching them to put them all back in.

Dogs love routine. I used to have an old girl that if I didn't have her dinner bowl down at 5:30 p.m., plus or minus about two minutes, she would start barking until I gave her food!

One of my current dogs, Sydney, insists on being fed first. As soon as she hears me in the kitchen with the dog bowls, she starts barking.

Jamie, my Gordon setter, howls for about two minutes every Sunday morning when I put him out in the kennel usually because I'm going out for an early Sunday breakfast. He's letting me know he really wants to be in the house and not in the ken-nel. He has gotten the rest of them to join in, and we call it Sunday service with the Gordon Tabernacle Choir.

The first time I took Patrick out for training on birds. He smelled, found, and pointed a bird. Then he looked at me as if to say, "Come over here and see what I found. What do I do now?" He gently picked up the bird, ran to me, and gave me the bird. He was very pleased with what he had found. He never barked, just looked up at me.

When the girls are in season, the intact males have one mission. Communication is difficult and reactions sometimes unpredictable. I do not trust the males with any wait or stay commands and have to carefully manage behaviors during this time.

Most sporting dogs, like the Irish setter, have high prey drives. All of mine are in the field hunting as well as training for obedience. A bird ten feet away, especially on an unseasoned youngster, is *always* going to be more interesting than the "wait" command while you flush the bird. Some might think this is an obvious miscommunication between the dog and handler, but the trick is to teach them that after they do wait, they get a reward. It might be chasing the bird, retrieving a bird, carrying a favorite toy around, a cookie. Different in different situations.

A good example of handler error or miscommunication with a dog while I was in the field was with my Kelly, who is now 10.5 years old. She was a puppy, maybe 12 to 14 months old, and would find the birds at hunt tests and pretty much clean out the field, but I couldn't get her to hold the points long enough. For the longest time, I couldn't figure out why sometimes she would hold it and sometimes not. An old timer came up to me at a hunt test and finally "trained" me. I had asked her to find the bird and then wait. But as she was pointing and locked in on the bird, I crossed over straight to the bird and broke her visual (line of sight) of the bird. She thought I was stealing her bird! As soon as I stopped doing that, guess what, she held the point. It took a long time to figure out I was the problem, not her!

If you have a sight hound, such as a greyhound or Afghan hound, your dog might enjoy lure coursing. With lure coursing, a piece of plastic is dragged quickly along a wire for the dogs to try to catch. The event generally takes place outside because of the speed of the dogs and how much room they require. The AKC and the American Sighthound Field Association offer these events. The idea is to mimic hunting conditions without using animals as prey. The dogs do not seem to mind that they are chasing a piece of plastic. They enjoy the chase. Your sight hound can earn titles at these events.

Coursing is different. In coursing, the sight hounds hunt down their prey, such as jackrabbits or hares. The dogs do enjoy it. Many sight hounds are quite good at catching a rabbit for dinner.

Therapy Dogs

Therapy dogs provide comfort and support to people in nursing homes, schools, hospitals, retirement homes, and other places they visit. They often help relieve stress and help people feel better. They sometimes visit the scene of a disaster and allow people to hug them. Therapy dogs do not have to be a certain breed. Any dog can become a therapy dog. They can be male or female, large or small. They do have to have a good temperament and be friendly. They must be patient and gentle. They must have good social skills and behave well in situations that might upset other dogs. It is important that they like being petted and handled even when the elderly or children who might be clumsy pet them. And they should be steady when they are around equipment such as wheelchairs and hospital equipment. They have to allow physical contact so the people they visit will feel better.

The requirements to become a therapy dog can vary depending on the organization you work with. There are two different national organizations that certify therapy dogs: Pet Partners® (formerly Delta Society) and Therapy Dogs International. Some schools, hospitals, libraries, and other places that use therapy dogs will accept certification from these two groups as proof that your dog is well behaved and knows how to be a good therapy dog. However, other schools, hospitals, and places have their own rules about therapy dogs and who can visit.

Despite these differences, most of the requirements for therapy dogs are similar. If your dog can pass the AKC's Canine Good Citizen program, he should be able to pass any requirements. Your dog should be able to cope with unexpected noise; deal with umbrellas, canes, wheelchairs, or people who walk oddly; be able to walk on surfaces he is unfamiliar with; accept friendly petting and hugs; and get along well with children and seniors. The requirements for the Canine Good Citizen test are located here: **www.akc.org/events/cgc/training_testing.cfm**.

If you would like to train for the Canine Good Citizen test, you can contact your local kennel club, dog training club, or animal shelter. They sometimes offer classes to help people and their dogs train for the test. Local pet stores with training classes also might offer classes to train for the test.

You can find out more information about Therapy Dogs International and their test by visiting their site: **www.tdi-dog.org/HowToJoin.aspx?Page=Testing+ Requirements**.

For information about the Pet Partners and their testing requirements you can visit their site: **https://www.petpartners.org**.

Therapy dogs perform an important service in their community by helping people when they are most vulnerable. Many people and their dogs help others by becoming a therapy dog team.

Search and Rescue Work

If you are interested in performing search and rescue work with your dog, know that it takes a lot of time, training, dedication, and, yes, money, to train your dog to become a search and rescue (SAR) dog. According to experts, the best SAR dogs are purebred dogs that come from a working, herding, or sporting breed. These breeds have good noses, and they have a strong prey drive that can be tweaked into  searching and finding what they are looking for. It is also good if you can start with a young puppy from a good breeder, and even better if the puppy comes from a family of dogs that has already proven that it has talent and ability for search and rescue work or tracking. Finding the right dog for search and rescue work can be the most important thing you do.

If you already have a dog, your dog possibly could make a good SAR dog. However, in some cases, the dog might be too old to start the training or have the wrong temperament, or he might not be interested in the work.

There are no regularly prescribed training methods for search and rescue dogs. Different groups or organizations train dogs and their handlers in different ways. The most popular training method is for an owner and dog to join a search team and train the dog slowly, usually training one day per week, and attending seminars, watching videos, and visiting other trainers occasionally. This method usually costs the owner less money. Unfortunately, with this method, dogs are in various stages of training all the time. If the team is needed for search and rescue, they might not have any well-trained, qualified teams able to respond.

Another method for training is to find a trainer willing to guarantee his work and training methods. He or she should be able to offer annual certification training so all of your team members and their dogs can attend the course at the same time. This method is much more expensive, so money has to be raised to pay for this training.

There are no minimum training standards for search and rescue dogs in the United States. The Federal Emergency Management Agency (FEMA) has a program for standard training, but it is not required. The Royal Canadian Mounted Police govern SAR dog standards in all provinces except Ontario and Quebec, but these are the only two standards offered in North America. Otherwise, states, counties, and other jurisdictions usually depend on calling in whoever has search and rescue dogs in their area. According to experts, this is a serious problem with search and rescue dog training, and it needs to be addressed in the future so there is a set standard for dogs and handlers.

Other Canine Jobs

Dogs always have done lots of jobs. They have herded, guarded, and hunted for us, as well as carried heavy loads and pulled carts, to name just a few of their jobs. Today there are fewer dogs on farms and doing work they used to do, but that does not mean they do not have jobs. They have adapted and have lots of new jobs in urban society.

Among the new jobs dogs have in the 21st century are IED and bomb-sniffing dogs, arson detection dogs, bedbug detection dogs, narcotics dogs, autism dogs, cancer detection dogs, diabetes detection dogs, and contraband dogs. And the list goes on. If people need to find something, the best way to find it is to use a dog. The dog's nose is so sensitive that no man-made machine can match it. Airport scanners are not as sensitive as a dog's nose when searching for terrorists. Dogs can find diseases hiding in the human body that doctors and medical testing will not find for months. Thus, dogs give patients a much better chance of survival. Children who cannot break out of the isolation of autism can hug and pet a dog.

We rely on dogs today as much as ever in terms of work and the things we need. As we continue to learn about all the wonderful things dogs can do, it seems that they always will have jobs.

Communicating with Senior Dogs

As your dog gets older, you probably will notice some changes in his demeanor. Some of the changes might be quite obvious, while others may be subtler. Age-related changes usually affect a dog's senses. Dogs can begin to lose their hearing, their eyesight can dim, and their senses of taste and smell will not be as strong as they once were. All of these changes can mean you could find your normal ways of communicating with your dog no longer work as well.

Changes to Your Dog's Senses

Just as with humans, your dog's senses can begin to diminish as he ages. This is normal, but it can mean you will need to find some new ways to communicate with your dog because the ways you have used do not work as well any longer.

For example, if you normally call your dog in for dinner, he might not come when you call him because his hearing is not as good as he gets older. You could need to compensate by going outside to get him or standing outside to make eye contact with him when you call him.

In some cases, if your dog is losing his hearing, you could teach him hand signals for commands. This is often done for deaf dogs and can allow you to continue to communicate.

CASE STUDY: CAROL AND REBA

Carol Ashley
Park Rapids, Minnesota

How many dogs do you have?

I have had dogs for all of my life, 60 years. I have one dog now, but I have had four others as an adult.

Some of the everyday words Reba knows are "walk," "sit," "down," "stay," "wait," "here" (come), "this way," "chicky bird," "turkey bird," "grouse bird," "rabbit," "chippy" (chipmunk), "on your chair," "on the bed," "in your crate," Kathy (neighbor), Rascal, Toby, Ella (dog buddies), "dinner," "lunch," "special food," "treat," and "cookie." Some of her understanding of specific words may be a bit questionable. I think some things she knows more by context than actual words.

I recognized at some point early on that she had a negative reaction to the word "come." This wasn't really miscommunication so much as it was a failure in understanding how to communicate with her my desire that she come. I started using "here," and though it took her some time to learn that coming to me did not mean punishment, it worked and eventually, after many years, she even lost her fear of the word "come."

About five months after I rescued Reba, and after she had gotten loose a couple of times, I had enlarged her pen, and she still managed to get out. She came running around me but not close enough for me to catch her. She kept running excitedly but not leaving. I still think she was telling me that she understood this was home and that she wasn't planning on running away but wanted to be able to be out of the pen and running around with me and George. Before that she always seemed to be heading for open land more like what she had grown up with.

It's rarely just the dog's look that gives me the clues as to what she wants but rather a mixture of all her body language. When she wants off the bed at night to head to her crate, she has an ears down, direct but soft stare. When she wants out, she comes to me and then paces back and forth until I get it. When she wants me to get moving on her dinner, she will make little sighing noises and watch me while her head is between her paws. When she is bored, she will bite her legs.

She does one firm bark, repeated after a minute or so, when she wants to come in. Her bark when she finds skunks or porcupines is higher pitched than normal and a little frantic sounding. She will stop after a minute or so as she looks to the house to see if I am coming and then repeats until I come to see what she found. Her bark when she finds chipmunks is also high-pitched, but with a happier sound and often with longer pauses in between. Her bark when she sees deer is more like her come-in bark, but it doesn't last long because she won't chase the deer far. When some other person or dog comes into the yard, she will do a bark that is like her come-in bark in tone and pitch but keeps it up until I come out.

There is a repetitive but not fast or excited bark that dogs do when left out at night. I call it the lonely, "let me in" bark. There is the excited barks of dogs in the neighborhood when another dog is going past their homes, the warning, "this is mine" bark.

I would have liked more communication, not necessarily better, but Reba was very fearful of people when I got her, and my first priority was to get her anxiety level down. Reba is now older and is losing her hearing, so we are finding different ways to communicate.

An example is a recent episode when I realized Reba and I were having a hard time keeping track of each other on our walks (it was usually more her job because she did it so well) and that the problem was that she could no longer hear me. After a couple days or so, I remembered how she and her late buddy, George, would communicate on their morning outing. One would start down the driveway, lets say George, and he would go just a little way and stop to look back to see if Reba was coming. He would wait until he knew she was coming and then continue.

They would do this intermittently as they headed down the driveway to check the morning news. I started doing this with Reba, and I'd swear her eyes got brighter and the light went on. It worked, and we both use this technique to be sure we know where the other is. Up until this time, Reba would never wait for me on a trail. Now she will stop and look back and won't go ahead until she is sure I have seen her and am coming.

Pay attention to their language and how they interact with other dogs, and incorporate that body language into your communications as much as possible. For example, a turning away if they are too rambunctious seems to let them know you don't want to play that way. I always use hand signals along with words when training in case the dog loses hearing. It has also come in handy in other situations when I am at a distance. Talk to them when they are young about things they are interested in. If my dogs show interest in a track, I will say "rabbit" or "grouse bird" and in more rare cases add a "bad" to let them know it's something they should be careful around. That probably worked due to skunk and porcupine episodes, and I saw it work later with a coyote incident. When she wanted to check out some coyote tracks, I said "bad coyote" and Reba stopped to look at me and then came and stayed close to me.

Because the ability to read body language is so important to dogs, your dog might not be able to read your signals as well as he once did if his eyesight is dimming as he ages. If your dog knows you well, he will be able to anticipate many things you might want him to do, but be clear about your intentions at all times so he is not confused.

Author Experiences: Sami

Sami was my first successful show dog. When she came to live with me at 2 years old, she was already a show champion. She was beautiful, sweet, and gentle, and she quickly became a wonderful pet. I owed her a lot. She had three large litters for me with some terrific puppies that also went on to become show champions. She also produced dogs that became obedience dogs, agility, and rally dogs, and hunters.

Many English setters can be good in the field if they have the instincts to hunt. Sami came from dual champion lines, field and show. Sami was also important because she possessed every health clearance important in our breed. She lived a long, healthy life, but as she got older, she started having a few quirks. For one thing, if she was in another room, she would sometimes start barking, and I would have to go fetch her. If a dog was lying on the floor, she might bark, and I would need to come and walk her around him. And, most noticeably, she would go outside at night by walking down the deck stairs, but then she would stand out in the yard barking or she would refuse to come back inside. I began to fear that my sweet Sami might have canine dementia. But she seemed fine when I was around to help her. I thought she almost seemed to be trying to tell me something about what was going on with her.

It finally dawned on me that at Sami's age (she was 11 or 12 when this behavior started), her eyesight was probably failing. Once I considered that possibility, everything seemed to make sense. I walked outside with her at night, and I could see that the shadows on the stairs would make it difficult for her to see the steps. But if I walked with her, she had no problem coming inside. She probably did not want to step over a dog because she could not judge distances well anymore. And she might have barked for me when she was in other rooms because she could not see well to find her way. Sometimes looking at things from your dog's point of view can help you solve a communication problem.

Vision

As dogs get older, they often begin to lose their sight. They can have cataracts, problems seeing at night, or eye diseases. If you suspect your dog is having vision problems, take him to your vet. In some cases, there are treatments to restore a dog's vision. However, in many cases, you might not even realize your dog is losing his vision. Dogs are good at compensating for a loss of sight, especially if they have lived

in the same home for many years. Your dog probably knows his way around your house with his eyes closed. Unless he should stumble over something unexpected in his path, you might not realize he has any sight problems.

If your dog is having vision problems, you can help him by always making sure he hears you when you call him. If he does not come quickly when you call him, go find him. He might not be able to see his way. If he has trouble navigating steps, especially at night, guide him. If you are out walking together, you could attach a long leash or check cord to your dog so you stay connected. This can prevent him from becoming separated from you.

Just because your dog's vision is dimming does not mean that his quality of life has to diminish. You can find many ways to assist him.

Taste and smell

Dogs rely on taste and smell to arouse their appetite. In many cases, older dogs can begin to lose interest in their food because these senses have begun to weaken and the food isn't appealing to them. Older dogs can stop eating and begin to lose weight. You can make the food smell and taste better if you add something tasty to the kibble such as a topping of stew or some canned food. Warming the food before you give it to your dog will also make it smell and taste better and encourage an older dog to eat it.

Older dogs also can stop eating because they have dental problems, so if your senior dog stops eating, check his teeth. He could have a broken tooth or a tooth that that is causing him pain when he eats needs to be removed. Once a veterinarian cares for the tooth, your older dog should resume eating again.

Obviously, all of these issues related to food will have an affect if you are trying to train your dog, as your senior dog probably will not be interested in anything unless it is extremely tasty and smells good. Senior dogs are quite capable of continuing to train and compete in events at advanced ages, and they can earn titles in agility, rally, and field events when they are past 10 years old. But to keep dogs interested and fit at these older ages, you will need to be aware of the changes that are happening with them due to their age. Dogs have to enjoy the training and feel good to compete when they are older. They need an owner who is attuned to them.

Hearing

Many senior dogs begin to lose their hearing, as they get older. Some dogs are born deaf in one or both ears. Dogs can also lose their hearing from ear infections. There are some ways you can boost your communication with your dog if he has begun to lose his hearing. Some people teach their dogs using hand signs. You can make up your own hand signals or use hand signals

created by the Deaf Dog Education Action Fund (DDEAF) **www.deafdogs.org/training/signs.php#training**. Some people teach their dogs using American Sign Language. You can use whatever works for you and your dog. The important thing is to be able to communicate. Dogs rely on body language far more than words anyway, so they easily can learn sign language.

If your older dog is losing his hearing, you will need to make a few adjustments. Do not sneak up on him. You could startle him. If you have other pets, your senior dog might resent them coming up behind him, and he might snap at them occasionally. They probably do not mean any harm, but your senior dog does not hear them, and he could snap because he is startled. Senior dogs often sleep soundly because they do not hear the noises around them. If you need to call your dog, you might have to wake him gently by shaking him. When you are walking your dog, keep him near you because he will not be able to hear traffic and other sounds that could indicate danger.

Lots of senior dogs that have lost their hearing live long and happy lives. If your senior dog is losing his hearing, you can make some adjustments to make his life comfortable and continue to communicate well.

Joint problems

If your older dog is beginning to have joint problems such as arthritis, see your veterinarian. A good pain management medication can help a dog with joint problems, including some over-the-counter supplements such as Dog Gone Pain, Cosequin®, glucosamine, chondroitin, MSM, shark cartilage, green-lipped  mussels, and others. The effectiveness of some of these supplements has not been proven, but many dog owners swear they have helped their dogs. Massaging your dog's muscles and joints gently can help. Using heated dog beds also helps some dogs.

Signs that your dog could be suffering from joint problems include difficulty getting up and down from sleeping, difficulty climbing stairs, reluctance to exercise, moving slowly, and occasionally making small sounds of pain such as a yelp or whine. Joint pain is not usually constant, but it can hurt your dog when he moves.

If your dog is beginning to have problems walking, such as slipping or sliding in your home, there are things you can do to improve life for him. If you have hardwood floors, in particular, you can put down area rugs throughout your home with adhesive on the back so they do not slide. This will allow your dog to step on them without sliding. Hardwood floors can be hard for older dogs because they do not provide any traction. You also can purchase doggy boots for your older dog, either for all four paws or just the rear paws. These boots have Gore-Tex® traction on the bottom of the shoes. They provide good traction for senior dogs so they can walk without falling. They come in many different sizes. They are available from pet stores and from dog supply vendors online. Muttluks® makes some dog booties that are good for inside use and which have good insoles for traction.

Canine cognitive dysfunction (CDS)

Canine cognitive dysfunction syndrome is often referred to as canine dementia or doggy Alzheimer's. It is believed to have a different cause in dogs, but the effects are similar to dementia in humans. Symptoms include:

- Disorientation/confusion
- Changes in sleep and behavior
- Housetraining problems from a dog who has been housetrained for years
- Aloofness

For example, your dog might walk into a room and stand in the middle of the floor as though he has forgotten why he is there. He could continue to stand there for a long time. It might seem like he does not know what he should do next. You might have to go to him and move him. Or, your dog could walk into a wall, as though he does not see it, though his eyes are fine. A dog could go into a room in your house and begin to bark; he might act like he is lost. And he could be lost. In his mind, he might not know where he is or where you are.

Clearly, if your dog is suffering from canine cognitive dysfunction, you will have problems with communication. If you notice any of these symptoms in your older dog, take him to your veterinarian. Medication can stop the progression of the disease, and your dog should improve.

All dogs age, of course, but vet care today is so advanced that there are many ways of keeping your older dog fit and healthy for years. With a little luck, you should be able to enjoy good communication with your dog all of his life.

Author Experiences: Taylor

Taylor was a mushy boy. Male dogs often seem to be more affectionate than girls, at least in English setters. Girls can be more independent, but the boys want petting, and they will lay their heart at your feet. Taylor was Sami's son, and he was like his mother in many ways. He was gentle and sweet, and he had her big, soulful, dark eyes. I love to think of Taylor's eyes and how they would look at me with concern. When my mother died and I was feeling bad, it was Taylor who would lay next to me trying to make me feel better. He would wash away my tears. How can you explain the bond that exists between people and their dogs when a dog knows you are hurting and he wants to help you? I will always be grateful to Taylor for providing me with comfort during the times when I felt bad. Somehow, he always knew.

I probably owe Taylor my life, in a literal sense. I fell asleep one night with a candle burning, and it was Taylor who poked me and nudged me until I woke up. The room was already full of smoke. I walked into the next room, where the candle had been, and the entire wall was in flames. I got the dogs out of the house and managed to get the fire put out, but it was extremely frightening. If Taylor had not awakened me, I would have died in the house. The back door was open into the backyard while I was asleep so Taylor could have run outside at any time, but he chose to stay inside a burning house to try to wake me. What can you say about a dog like that, or how much we owe to dogs?

Saying Goodbye

Perhaps the hardest thing about having a dog is saying goodbye. You spend your life together, loving each other, working together, doing so many things together, building so many wonderful memories. But dogs never live as long as we do. There always comes a day when you have to let your friend go.

The same communication that has brought you and your dog so close together for years will also let you recognize when your dog is telling you that it is time to release him. Trust what your dog is telling you, and always do what is best for him. He will know that you are acting out of love. In time, your heart will heal, and you will be ready to have another best friend.

Conclusion

Good communication is the key to a good relationship with your dog. The better you understand what your dog is communicating and the better you are at communicating with your dog, the better you can understand each other. You can overcome nearly any problem when the two of you know what the other is thinking and feeling.

Communication takes work. No matter how many dogs you have had or how long you have "been in dogs," every dog is different, and they can express themselves differently.

Dogs are individuals, and dogs of different breeds react differently to things. They are not interchangeable. You cannot raise a Chihuahua puppy the same way you would raise an Akita puppy. They certainly share certain characteristics because they are both dogs but the wise owner will try to understand what each individual dog needs and tailor communication appropriately. Socialization will be different for different dogs. Training will need to be different. Even the dog's body language can be slightly different.

So, take the information provided in this book and use it as a starting point, but keep in mind that your own experiences with the dogs in your life will give you useful information as you move forward. Be adaptable as you work with different dogs.

It would be wonderful if every puppy got off to a great start in life and came from a great breeder who started his socialization early and prepared him to go to his new home, but that is not the case. Many puppies and dogs today come from pounds and shelters where they are already behind in socialization. When you bring one of these puppies or dogs home, he already might have some behavior problems that can range from minor (needing socialization) to remedial (need to learn to stop barking or jumping on people or to relearn housetraining). Keep this in mind when you work with these puppies and dogs, and try to be extra patient. Pounds and shelters should not be adopting out dogs with any major behavior problems, such as aggression. If you accidentally bring home a puppy or dog with such a problem, contact the shelter and consider returning the dog. It is not a good idea to bring home a new dog with a major behavior problem, especially if you have children.

Remember that your dog is communicating with you all the time. He is good at reading you and knowing what you are doing, saying, and even thinking. It is up to you to discover the things that your dog is communicating. If you learn to pay attention, you will discover your dog is telling you things by means of his body language and expressions every minute. The world is much richer when you understand what your dog is saying.

Appendix

Dog Training Resources

International Association of Animal Behavior Consultants (IAABC) http://iaabc.org

The International Association of Animal Behavior Consultants is a respected group of behavior consultants that works with many species, including dogs. Some of their consultants are dog trainers and veterinary behaviorists. They are particularly good at working with dogs that have serious problems such as difficult cases of separation anxiety and aggression. You can find a consultant in your area by visiting their site.

Association of Pet Dog Trainers (APDT) www.apdt.com

The Association of Pet Dog Trainers is a professional group of dog trainers with the stated goal of improving their training methods through education. The group was founded in 1993 by esteemed dog trainer Dr. Ian Dunbar. Today they have more than 6000 members all over the world. You can find a trainer in your area by visiting the site.

Suggested Reading

Aloff, Brenda. *Canine Body Language, A Photographic Guide: Interpreting The Native Language of the Domestic Dog.* Wenatchee, Washington: Dogwise, 2005.

Coppinger, Raymond. *Dogs: A New Understanding of Canine Origin, Behavior and Evolution.* Chicago: University of Chicago Press, 2002.

Coren, Stanley. *How To Speak Dog: Mastering the Art of Dog-Human Communication.* New York: Free Press, 2000.

Coren, Stanley. *The Intelligence of Dogs: A Guide To The Thoughts, Emotions, And Inner Lives Of Our Canine Companions.* New York: Bantam, 1995.

Hoffman, Matthew, ed. *Dogspeak: How To Understand Your Dog and Help Him Understand You.* Emmaus, Pennsylvania: Rodale Press, 1999.

Donaldson, Jean. *The Culture Clash: A Revolutionary New Way to Understanding the Relationship Between Humans and Domestic Dogs*. James & Kenneth, 1996.

Green, Susie. *Talk To Your Dog: How To Communicate With Your Pet*. New York: Sterling Publishing, 2005.

McConnell, Patricia B., Ph.D. *For the Love of a Dog*. New York: Ballantine, 2006.

McConnell, Patricia B., Ph.D. *The Other End of the Leash*. New York: Ballantine, 2002.

Millan, Cesar. *Cesar's Way: The Natural, Everyday Guide To Understanding & Common Dog Problems*. New York: Three Rivers Press, 2006.

Pryor, Karen. *Don't Shoot The Dog!: The New Art of Teaching and Training*. Ringpress Books, 2006.

Rugaas, Turid. *On Talking Terms With Dogs: Calming Signals*. Dogwise, 2005.

Scott, John Paul, and John L. Fuller. *Genetics and Social Behavior of the Dog*. Chicago: University of Chicago Press, 1998.

About the Author

Carlotta Cooper was born and raised in Tennessee. Her grandparents were farmers, and she grew up with horses, dogs, and other animals, including some pigs raised for the table. Her grandparents had their own smokehouse and cured their own meats. She attended the University of the South in Sewanee where she graduated with a B.A. in English as class salutatorian. She attended graduate school at the University of Virginia, studying English literature, and did graduate work in writing and rhetoric at the University of Tennessee at Chattanooga.

Professionally, Carlotta is a freelance writer, specializing in writing about animals. She has been breeding and showing dogs for more than 20 years. She has a contributing editor for the dog show magazine *Dog News*. She lives in the middle of farm country in Tennessee now, writing about veterinary issues, animal reproduction, genetics, and raising and caring for animals. Carlotta is now thinking of adding some Gloucestershire Old Spots to her home menagerie.

Index